FREE AND SUPER CHEAP CAMPING IN CALIFORNIA

ONE HUNDRED FIVE STAR CAMPSITES FOR NATIONAL FOREST CAMPING, BUREAU OF LAND MANAGEMENT, FEDERAL, STATE, COUNTY, RV CAMPING, TENT CAMPING, BOONDOCKING

FREE AND SUPER CHEAP CAMPING SERIES

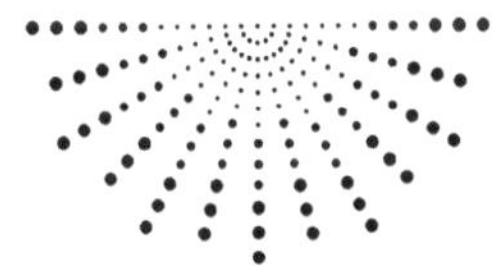

RICH SHIPLEY

WAYFARE ARTS, LLC

* * *

Cover photo by Rich Shipley. Mt. Whitney viewed through Mobius Arch. Alabama Hills, Lone Pine, CA.

FREE AND SUPER CHEAP CAMPING SERIES

FREE AND SUPER CHEAP CAMPING SERIES

The Free and Super Cheap Camping series is your passport to budget-friendly adventures across America's most beautiful public lands in:

COLORADO, UTAH, NEVADA, CALIFORNIA, OREGON, WASHINGTON, ARIZONA, NEW MEXICO

Each book features top-rated campsites, plus the tools and knowledge to help you discover thousands more. Whether you're camping in the mountains, by the sea, or in the desert, you'll find detailed information, GPS coordinates, maps, and tips to help you explore with confidence — all while keeping your travel costs low and your sense of freedom high.

SCAN OR CLICK BELOW TO SEE THE ENTIRE SERIES, AND START PLANNING YOUR NEXT CAMPING ADVENTURE.

Free and Super Cheap Camping Series: https://t2bk.com/ATT

CONTENTS

Introduction ix

1. NORTHERN CALIFORNIA 1
*** SHASTA TRINITY AREA *** 2
2. Douglas City Campground - $20/$10 2
3. Junction City Campground - $15/$7.50 3
4. Mad River Campground - $12/$6 4
5. Hayden Flat Campground - $12/$6 5
6. Pigeon Point Campground - $12/$6 6
7. Castle Lake Campground - FREE 7
8. Sand Flat Dispersed Camping - FREE 8
9. Algoma Campground - FREE 9
10. Curly Jack Campground - $15/$7.50 10
11. Beaver Creek Campground - FREE 11
12. Kangaroo Lake Campground $15/$7.50 12
13. Trail Creek Campground $10/$5 13
14. Deer Mountain Snowpark - FREE 14
*** LASSEN AND PLUMAS AREA *** 15
15. Hat Creek Campground - $16/$8 15
16. Domingo Springs Campground - $14/$7 16
17. Almanor Campground - $18/$9 17
18. Roxie Peconom Campground - FREE 18
19. Rocky Point East Campground - FREE 19
20. Fort Sage Trailhead Campsite - FREE 20
21. Indian Well Campground - $20/$10 21
22. Butte Meadows Campground - $12/$6 22
*** REDWOOD COAST *** 23
23. Mattole Beach Campground - $15/$7.50 23
24. Trinidad Southbound Rest Area - Free 24
25. Panther Flat Campground - $15/$7.50 25
26. Grassy Flat Campground - $10/$5 26

27. Bear River Casino – 72 hours free. 27
28. Jedediah Smith Campground - $35/$17.50 28
29. Swimmer's Delight Campground - $30 29

2. SIERRA NEVADA 30
••• TAHOE & SURROUNDING AREA ••• 31
31. Lakes Basin Recreation Area 31
32. Gold Lake Campground - $22/$11 32
33. Watson Lake Campground - FREE 33
34. Alpine Meadow Campground - $20/$10 34
35. Indian Valley Campground - $24/$12 35
36. Packsaddle Campground - $24/$12 36
37. Wild Plum Campground - $24/$12 37
38. Hope Valley SnoPark - FREE 38
39. Lindsey Lake Campground - $15 39
40. Cottonwood Creek Campground - $20/$10 40
••• YOSEMITE AREA ••• 41
41. Beardsley Dam Campground - $25/$12.50 41
42. Fraser Flat Campground $25/$12.50 42
43. Hardin Flat Road Dispersed Campsites - FREE 43
44. Sweetwater Campground - $29/$14.50 44
••• EASTERN SIERRA ••• 45
45. Alabama Hills, Movie Flat Designated Dispersed Camping - FREE 45
46. Tuttle Creek Campground - $10/$5 46
47. Green Creek Road Dispersed Camping - FREE 47
48. Aspen Campground - $14/$7 48
49. Tioga Lake Campground - $28/$14 49
50. Glass Creek Campground - FREE 50
51. Lower Lee Vining Campground - $14/$7 51
52. Mono Creek Campground $35/$17.50 52
53. Owens River Rd Dispersed Camping - FREE 53
54. Crowley Lake Campground - $10/$5 54
55. Mammoth Lakes Scenic Loop – FREE 55

56. Taboose Creek Campground - $14 56
57. Sagehen Meadows Campground - FREE 57

3. CENTRAL CALIFORNIA 58
••• CENTRAL COAST ••• 59
59. Cerro Alto Campground - $35/$17.50 59
60. Benicia EnRoute Camp - $12 60
61. Morro Bay State Park Campground - $35 61
62. Williams Hill Recreation Area - FREE 62
63. Sugarloaf Ridge State Park - $35 63
*** SEQUOIA & KINGS CANYON ••• 64
64. Princess Campground - $34/$17 64
65. Western Big Meadow Road Camping Area - FREE 65
66. Redwood Meadow Campground - $34/$17 66
67. Upper Stony Creek Campground - $34/$17 67
••• CENTRAL VALLEY ••• 68
68. Kirch Flat Campground - FREE 68
69. Acorn Campground - $20/$10 69
70. Condon Peak Campground - $5 permit 70
71. McCabe Flat Campground - $10/$5 71
72. Buckhorn Recreation Area - $20/$10 72
73. Carnegie SVRA - $10 73
74. Hollister Hills SVRA - $10 74
75. Selby Campground - FREE 75
76. KCL Campground - FREE 76
77. Upper Sweetwater Campground - FREE 77

4. SOUTHERN CALIFORNIA 78
79. Guajome Regional Park - $33 79
80. William Heise County Park Campground - $29 80
81. Horse Flats Campground - $12/$6 81
82. Aliso Park Campground - FREE 82
83. Ogilby Road Dispersed Camping - FREE 83
84. Old Isabella Road Recreation Site - $12/$6 84
85. Mt. Pinos Campground - $30/$15 85

86. Crystal Lake Campground - $12/$6 86
87. Mountain Oak Campground - $30/$15 87
88. Reyes Creek Campground - $30/$15 88
89. Campo Alto Campground - $30/$15 89
90. Coon Creek Yellow Post Campsites - FREE 90
••• MOJAVE DESERT ••• 91
91. Silurian Dry Lake Bed - FREE 91
92. Trona Pinnacles - FREE 92
93. Owl Canyon Campground - $6/$3 93
94. Kelso Dunes Mine - FREE 94
95. Mid Hills Campground - $20/$10 95
96. Fossil Falls Dry Lake Bed - FREE 96
97. Amboy Crater - FREE 97
98. Little Cowhole Mountain - FREE 98
••• DEATH VALLEY AREA ••• 99
99. Wildrose Campground - FREE 99
100. Stovepipe Wells Campground - $14/$7 100
101. Furnace Creek Road Dispersed Camping - FREE 101
••• JOSHUA TREE AREA ••• 102
102. Joshua Tree South Dispersed Camping - FREE 102
103. Belle Campground - $25/$12.50 103

5. BLM WINTER AND SUMMER LONG-TERM VISITOR AREAS 104
There are Seven winter LTVAs 104
There are Four Summer LTVAs in California 105

6. RESOURCES 107
Resources for thousands of great places to camp 107
Government websites for further research 108

7. THANK YOU! 109

INTRODUCTION

Until recently, I was living and traveling in various campers/RVs full time for almost 7 years. 95% of that time, I camped in great free or cheap places. If that sounds good, or if you want to learn about some beautiful places to camp and not spend a fortune just to be camped ridiculously close to your neighbor, follow along.

Hopefully, this book will give you some great ideas of where you might like to camp. By no means is this an exhaustive list! It's an excellent starter list, and at the end of the book, I will point you to resources with thousands of other great places to camp. More places than you could get to in a lifetime. For this book, I concentrate on some places where other campers and I have given very high ratings. I won't be including RV parks or the higher-cost campgrounds. Those are not my thing, so I can't advise you on those places, but they can be found in the resources listed at the end of the book if you're interested.

Regarding the ratings, what I, or some other people, consider a highly rated campsite may or may not be your cup of tea, or it might not be suitable for your vehicle or your camping style. Many types of camp areas are listed, from sites suitable for tents only to sites that can accommodate large RVs and motorhomes. Sites with amenities and sites with no facilities at all. A few sites might require a high clearance or a 4WD vehicle. Please read the listings, then do some internet research on your own to learn what you can about a potential camp area to better understand what to expect.

Each camping area listed will give you the name, whether it's free or low cost (at the time of writing), general location, GPS coordinates, the managing agency (forest service, BLM, etc.), and a brief description. **Again, once you've found something interesting, the next step in your planning would be to look the campground up by name or city/area on Google or one of the websites or apps listed at the end of this book. Please do your research!** It's always best to check these to ensure you have the latest info in case of closures, rough or washed-out roads, or whatever. You'll also find more reviews on these sites and info on cell service availability, elevation, etc.

Many sites listed are first-come, first-serve, while others can be reserved. Here are the common reservation websites.

www.recreation.gov For most federal lands campgrounds.

www.reserveamerica.com for state and regional parks.

Do an internet search for county park reservations.

HOW TO USE THIS BOOK

For each campground listed, you will see links and QR codes. Depending on if you are reading the paperback or a Kindle or mobile device, you can click on a link or scan the QR code with your phone camera.

Photos: https://t2bk.com/YE

Here's a QR code example. Go ahead and try it out now.

AND FINALLY, A NOTE ABOUT THE PRICES LISTED

Most of the campgrounds listed are managed by the National Forest Service or Bureau of Land Management. On the campgrounds with two prices, the lower price is if you have an annual or senior pass. Information on those passes is available at the end of this book.

INTERACTIVE MAP. SCROLL AND ZOOM.

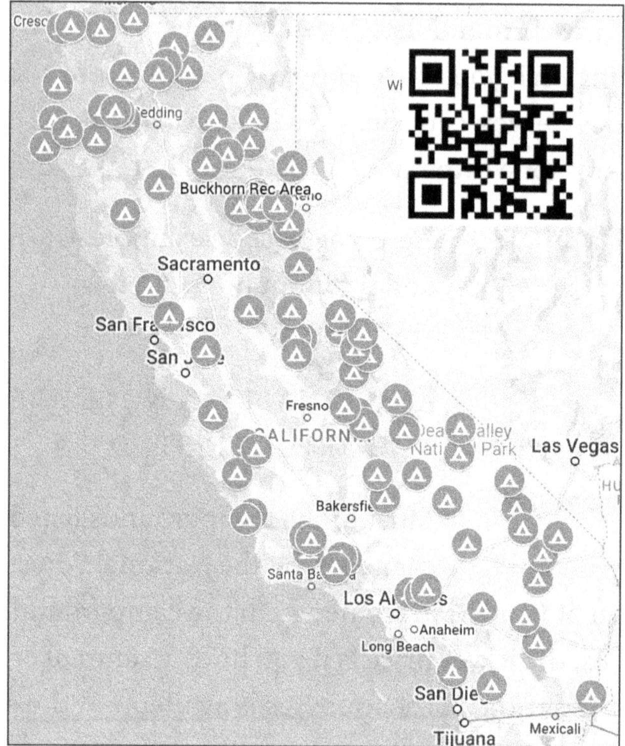

Map: https://t2bk.com/YF

Site names/numbers on the online map correspond to site names/numbers in the book.

Ok, enough said...

LET'S GO CAMPING!

1

NORTHERN CALIFORNIA

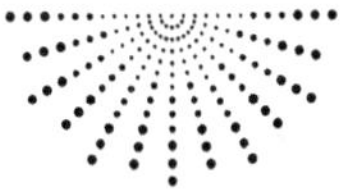

*** SHASTA TRINITY AREA ***

2. DOUGLAS CITY CAMPGROUND - $20/$10

- BLM
- On the Trinity River
- Douglas City, CA
- GPS: 40.648, -122.954

Map: https://t2bk.com/YG

This section of the river is well-known for its world-class fly fishing and is a popular destination among anglers and pleasure boaters alike. The pristine, cold water of the river is a favorite spot for paddlers who enjoy exploring the narrow valley, which is flanked by canyons adorned with Ponderosa Pine, Douglas Fir, Oaks, and Madrone trees.

Photos: https://t2bk.com/YH

The campground has potable water, a vault toilet, showers, and bear boxes. It's a nice campground within driving distance of many good hiking trails. The bathrooms and showers are clean. Each site has a picnic table, a bear box, and a fire pit. There's access to the river right on the campgrounds, and you can hear the water from everywhere. Sites are mostly private, wooded, and clean, and some are on the river. Excellent RV, tent, and car camping.

3. JUNCTION CITY CAMPGROUND - $15/$7.50

- BLM
- CA-Hwy 299
- Junction City, CA
- GPS: 40.7464, -123.0638

Maps: https://t2bk.com/YI

Junction City Campground is located off Highway 299, west of Weaverville, CA, and is an excellent place to take a break during long drives. Expect some road noise. It's a popular spot for both fishing and pleasure boating. The Trinity River has clear waters and is famous for fly fishing. Paddlers can enjoy the beautiful canyons with Ponderosa Pine, Douglas fir, oaks, and madrone trees.

Photos: https://t2bk.com/YJ

The Trinity River's waters below Pigeon Point offer class III-V rapids for whitewater enthusiasts and those seeking an adrenaline rush. This stretch of the river also has hiking trails and opportunities for swimming, fishing, and gold panning. The campground is open from May to November on a first-come, first-served basis. Facilities include vault toilets, bear boxes, and potable water.

4. MAD RIVER CAMPGROUND - $12/$6

- Six Rivers National Forest
- Lower Mad River Road
- Mad River, CA
- GPS: 40.403, -123.466

Map: https://t2bk.com/YK

This quiet and under-used campground has 40 campsites in a picturesque setting. Tucked beneath the shade of Douglas fir, maples, and manzanita trees, it's a beautiful and quiet area for campers. Some campsites have direct access to the river via nearby trails. First come, first served with self-registration at the entrance kiosk, no reservations. The campsite allows campers to stay for a maximum of 14 days and permits leashed pets.

Mad River Campground has well-maintained sites with fire rings, picnic tables, and access to running water. The restrooms are kept clean. Some campsites are near the river, and Ruth Lake is just a short drive away. Because of the rocky bottom, it is advisable to bring water shoes for wading in the river.

Photos: https://t2bk.com/AAE

5. HAYDEN FLAT CAMPGROUND - $12/$6

- On the Trinity River
- Shasta Trinity National Forest
- Big Bar, CA
- GPS: 40.739, -123.203

Map: https://t2bk.com/YM

Hayden Flat is a small campground with riverfront campsites and one of the best beaches on the Trinity River. It's located in the Wild and Scenic section of the river. The upper loop of the campground has been converted into three group sites. The Trinity River offers fishing, swimming, floating, rafting, kayaking, and boating—easy river access for boats that can be hand-carried. Nearby creeks and streams provide more beautiful spots to swim and spend the day.

Hayden Flat Campground is open year-round, but the upper group campground is only open from Memorial Day to Labor Day. There are vault toilets and trash and recycling facilities, but no potable water is provided on-site. The only downside is some noise from the highway.

Photos: https://t2bk.com/YN

6. PIGEON POINT CAMPGROUND - $12/$6

- Shasta National Forest
- On the Trinity River
- Highway 299
- Big Bar, CA
- GPS: 40.767, -123.13

Map: https://t2bk.com/YO

On CA Highway 299, about 15 miles west of Weaverville, CA, the campground is right on the beautiful Trinity River with good river access. It is a popular spot for rafters and kayakers to access the river. There is some highway noise. Reservations for groups only. Non-potable water. The facility has a self-registration/fee station at the entrance and convenient river access.

This campground is located on the Wild and Scenic portion of the Trinity River. It's a beautiful place to camp and enjoy the river's many amenities. Sites are first-come, first-served and open seasonally from late May through early October, weather permitting. Campers must bring all supplies and pack out waste.

Photos: https://t2bk.com/YP

7. CASTLE LAKE CAMPGROUND - FREE

- Shasta National Forest
- Castle Lake Road
- Mount Shasta, CA
- GPS: 41.236, -122.379

Map: https://t2bk.com/YQ

Castle Lake Campground is a primitive campground in a dense forest a quarter mile from Castle Lake. It has only six sites, each with a table, a fire ring, and access to vault toilets. Bring your own water. The campground has a three-night stay limit, no reservations, and is not suitable for large vehicles or trailers. It usually opens in late May and closes with the first snowfall in November.

Photos: https://t2bk.com/YR

A short walk or drive to Castle Lake, a crystal-clear glacial cirque lake ringed by granite cliffs. Castle Lake is perfect for hiking, swimming, fishing, and kayaking on its calm waters. Several hiking trails are available, including the easy Shoreline Trail on the west side of the lake or the more challenging hike up to Heart Lake, which provides a fantastic view over Castle Lake.

8. SAND FLAT DISPERSED CAMPING - FREE

- Shasta National Forest
- Sand Flat Rd.
- Mount Shasta, CA
- GPS: 41.3539, -122.2497

Map: https://t2bk.com/YS

Dispersed camping. This is not a campground. This location has stunning views of Mount Shasta and is best accessed via Lower Sand Flat Road. You'll find plenty of camping choices in the area. It's advisable to use a high-clearance vehicle if you're aiming to reach the more secluded spots. Be aware that Upper Sand Flat Road has rough ruts and gullies.

Photos: https://t2bk.com/YT

You can find something suitable whether you prefer camping in full sunlight or a shaded spot among the trees. The Sand Flat region has numerous dispersed camping spots, offering breathtaking views of Casaval Ridge and Mount Shasta. You'll be surrounded by towering Shasta Red Fir trees, vibrant green moss, and an atmosphere of peace and tranquility. Do not create new camping sites or drive into Sand Flat proper, as doing so could result in a citation.

9. ALGOMA CAMPGROUND - FREE

- Shasta National Forest
- Volcanic Legacy Scenic Byway
- McCloud, CA
- GPS: 41.2561, -121.8833

Map: https://t2bk.com/YU

This spot might be perfect if you're looking for a campground near the McCloud River. Only eight sites are available, and the campground can get a bit noisy and crowded on the weekends because of the influx of locals. Don't let that deter you from visiting the nearby McCloud Falls, which is a must-see. The forest setting provides peaceful opportunities for birdwatching, hiking, and enjoying quiet mornings immersed in nature.

Photos: https://t2bk.com/YW

The campground contains 30 individual sites suitable for tents and small to mid-size RVs, each equipped with a picnic table and fire ring. Vault toilets are available; there is no potable water on site. Sites are first-come, first-served and generally open from late May through early October, depending on snowpack. There are no hookups or dump stations. Campers must bring all their supplies, pack out all waste, and follow Leave No Trace principles.

10. CURLY JACK CAMPGROUND - $15/$7.50

- Klamath National Forest
- Curly Jack Rd.
- Happy Camp, CA
- GPS: 41.7851, -123.3897

Map: https://t2bk.com/YX

Curly Jack Campground, located in the legendary Bigfoot country, is just a short walk from Happy Camp on the banks of the Klamath River. This scenic spot offers 16 large campsites arranged in a paved loop under a canopy of trees alongside the river. The spacious sites provide easy river access and ensure a mix of sun and shade.

Each campsite at Curly Jack has a fire pit and potable water. The campground also has clean vault toilets. It's ideal for water enthusiasts, offering swimming, rafting, and fishing opportunities. This campground is a little slice of secluded paradise tucked away among the hills and rivers of Northern California, perfect for a tranquil getaway.

Photos: https://t2bk.com/YY

11. BEAVER CREEK CAMPGROUND - FREE

- Klamath National Forest
- Forest Route 48N01
- Klamath River, CA
- GPS: 41.927, -122.829

Map: https://t2bk.com/YZ

Beaver Creek Campground offers a secluded camping experience alongside Beaver Creek. It's an excellent spot for trout fishing, but remember to check the current regulations, as fishing is sometimes restricted. The campground has a dirt/gravel parking area with several flat spaces suitable for camp setup. There's also a clean and relatively new pit toilet on-site. Quigley's Store on Hwy 96 is just 5 miles away for groceries and a coffee fix. Yreka is a 30-minute drive, and Happy Camp is a bit further west.

Potos: https://t2bk.com/ZA

This tranquil, remote campground beside a beautiful stream is perfect for peace and tranquility. The road going past gets very little traffic. Whether you're here to camp overnight or to spend a relaxing day by the creek, Beaver Creek Campground is an excellent choice.

12. KANGAROO LAKE CAMPGROUND $15/$7.50

- Shasta National Forest
- Rail Creek Road
- Gazelle, CA 96034
- GPS: 41.335, -122.641

Map: https://t2bk.com/ZB

This pristine mountain lake campground has around 20 drive-in and walk-in sites. Nearby hiking trails offer incredible views that are perfect for stargazing. The campground is quiet and wheelchair-accessible, providing beautiful scenery and access to the PCT and other trails.

Fishing from the shore or rowboat is ideal, as motorized boats are prohibited. The access road can be narrow in places, but it's worth the drive. The best time to secure a spot is on weekdays, first come, first served. It's a great place to relax, fish, and hike. It can get busy on weekends and holidays.

Photos: https://t2bk.com/ZC

13. TRAIL CREEK CAMPGROUND $10/$5

- Klamath National Forest
- Fh 903
- Forks of Salmon, CA
- GPS: 41.229, -122.972

Map: https://t2bk.com/ZD

The remote Trail Creek Campground is on the East Fork of the South Fork Salmon River. It has twelve well-shaded campsites, vault toilets, potable water, and bear-proof trash receptacles. The campground is an excellent spot for outdoor activities, and there are more opportunities for hiking and fishing in the nearby Trinity Alps and Russian Wilderness Area. Note: Towing trailers is not recommended when heading west from Cecilville, although the road from Callahan to Cecilville is passable.

This campground is at higher elevation and has cooler nighttime temperatures than nearby areas. Trail Creek is a lightly used campground and provides a peaceful setting for campers to enjoy the surroundings and the proximity to the Salmon River.

Photos: https://t2bk.com/ZE

14. DEER MOUNTAIN SNOWPARK - FREE

- Klamath National Forest
- Forest Route 42N12
- Weed, CA
- GPS: 41.5705, -122.132

Map: https://t2bk.com/ZF

Deer Mountain Snow Park has eight campsites and five picnic areas. It's popular in the summer and has a cozy warming hut and snowmobile trails for winter fun. The campsites are flat and paved, each with a picnic table and fire pit. There's no garbage service or water, so come prepared. The sites are spacious and spread out, making them suitable for big rigs.

You can camp here for up to 14 days at no charge. Every campsite has its own fire pit and picnic table, with plenty shaded by trees. It's a great, quiet, and safe location for families, with lots of space for kids to play. If you're into solar, a snow park across the street gets lots of sun.

Photos: https://t2bk.com/ZG

*** LASSEN AND PLUMAS AREA ***

15. HAT CREEK CAMPGROUND - $16/$8

- Lassen National Forest
- State Highway 89
- Old Station, CA
- GPS: 40.668, -121.447

Map: https://t2bk.com/ZH

Hat Creek Campground, located in a mixed coniferous forest next to Hat Creek, offers excellent stream fishing with trophy trout. Across the road, you'll find the scenic Spatter Cones Trail. Just a mile north, the adventurous Subway Cave lava tube is worth a visit. There are access stairs to the cave, but you'll need a strong flashlight and sturdy shoes! For area information, check out the Old Station Visitor Information Center.

Flowing right by the campground, Hat Creek is renowned for world-class trout fishing. It's approximately 4,400-foot elevation and provides cooler temperatures than lower valley locations.

Photos: https://t2bk.com/ZI

16. DOMINGO SPRINGS CAMPGROUND - $14/$7

- Lassen National Forest
- Old Red Bluff Rd
- Chester, CA
- GPS: 40.3605, -121.3474

Map: https://t2bk.com/ZJ

Domingo Springs Campground offers 18 sites on a first-come, first-served basis, each equipped with campfire rings and tables. The local Maidu Indians once revered this spot as the "center of the universe." There's a lovely meadow right by the campground, and across the road, you'll find the spring's source, which forms a beautiful water garden. A pipe offers fresh spring water to refill your jugs and water bottles.

The campground is alongside a marshy creek fed by the spring. The creek flows through the campground, dividing the main area from a few smaller sites on the other side. A footbridge links these two sections. The Pacific Crest Trail crosses the road roughly 1,500 feet west of the campground entrance.

Photos: https://t2bk.com/ZK

17. ALMANOR CAMPGROUND - $18/$9

- Lassen National Forest
- Almanor Drive West
- Canyondam, CA
- GPS: 40.2176, -121.1764

Map: https://t2bk.com/ZL

Almanor Campground, ideal for both families and groups, lies on the west shore of Lake Almanor at 4,540 feet elevation amidst a scenic mixed conifer forest with shaded areas and wild-flower-filled meadows. This family-friendly facility offers a variety of activities, including boating, swimming, water skiing, and sailing on the 28,000-acre lake. A boat ramp is available at the north campground. Fishing for trout, bass, salmon, and catfish is popular. The Dixie Fire came close but did not burn into the campground.

Photos: https://t2bk.com/ZM

The Lake Almanor Recreation Trail provides excellent views along the lake's west shore. Campsites here are suitable for tents and RVs (no hookups), have tables and campfire rings, with vault toilets and drinking water available. Parking is limited. First-come, first-served.

18. ROXIE PECONOM CAMPGROUND - FREE

- Lassen National Forest
- Susanville, CA
- GPS: 40.3544, -120.8097

Map: https://t2bk.com/ZN

Roxie Pencom Campground is 2 miles off Highway 36 and offers rustic and peaceful camping with its 10 first-come, first-served sites. Pack it in, pack it out. You'll find hand-pumped water and a vault toilet, with the restrooms kept nice and clean. The campground is serene, close to Willard Creek, and you might even spot some bear and raccoon tracks by the creek.

Photos: https://t2bk.com/ZO

The campground is wooded, and there's a nice picnic area with about eight picnic tables arranged spaciously around a grove. The layout forms a wide open circle around a small cluster of trees, offering a mix of sunny and shaded spots. There aren't any clearly marked sites. The local Maidu Indian tribe uses this area for their gatherings and ceremonies. Please be respectful and take all of your trash with you.

19. ROCKY POINT EAST CAMPGROUND - FREE

- BLM
- Rocky Point Access Rd.
- Susanville, CA
- GPS: 40.6729, -120.7459

Map: https://t2bk.com/ZP

Rocky Point East Campground sits on the eastern shore of Lake Almanor near Susanville, California, at about 4,600 feet elevation. The setting is a pine and cedar forest with open understory, offering shaded and sunny spots. From many sites you can see the lake through the trees, and a nearby trail leads down to the water's edge. Common wildlife includes deer, chipmunks, and songbirds; bald eagles and ospreys are occasionally seen fishing over the lake.

The area has room to spread out and enjoy privacy, with few neighbors in sight. However, the road leading to Rocky Point East is rough and not suited for very large vehicles. Each site has a picnic table and fire ring. Vault toilets are provided, but there is no potable water or hookups. Sites are available on a first-come, first-served basis.

Photos: https://t2bk.com/ZQ

20. FORT SAGE TRAILHEAD CAMPSITE - FREE

- Fort Sage OHV Area
- Fort Sage Road
- Doyle, CA
- GPS: 40.06, -120.0725

Map: https://t2bk.com/ZR

The Fort Sage Off-Highway Vehicle Area is in northeastern California's high desert. To get there, use Laver Crossing Road, as there's a weight restriction on the bridge off Doyle Loop Road. This remote location is a hidden gem known for its well-maintained campsites and tranquil environment. You'll likely see cattle and deer roaming around. Clean bathrooms, quiet setting, and stunning sunset views.

Photos: https://t2bk.com/ZS

This area includes three separate parking areas, each with bathroom facilities. You'll find spectacular views, vault toilets, trash cans, fire pits with grills, and picnic tables. The dirt road is well-kept, allowing easy access even for big rigs. With two small camping areas, there's enough space to accommodate 10-12 vehicles of any size. For adventure seekers, there are plenty of OHV trails to explore. It can get busy on weekends.

21. INDIAN WELL CAMPGROUND - $20/$10

- Lava Beds National Monument
- Lava Beds Campground Rd.
- Tulelake, CA
- GPS: 41.7173, -121.5042

Map: https://t2bk.com/ZT

Indian Well Campground lies just ½ mile from the Lava Beds Visitor Center within Lava Beds National Monument. This family-style campground offers 43 first-come, first-served sites and a separate group site available by reservation. Sites accommodate tents, pickup campers, small trailers, and motorhomes up to 30 feet. Each site includes a picnic table, fire ring with grill, and paved parking pad—either back-in or pull-through depending on the loop. Vault (flush) toilets and potable drinking water are available; there are no showers or RV hookups.

This campground is an excellent base for exploring lava tube caves like Mushpot and Catacombs via short trails, with abundant wildlife including deer and songbirds nearby. A self-registration permit is required within 30 minutes of arrival at the kiosk.

Photos: https://t2bk.com/ZU

22. BUTTE MEADOWS CAMPGROUND - $12/$6

- Lassen National Forest
- Skyway Rd.
- Butte Meadows, CA
- GPS: 40.078, -121.559

Map: https://t2bk.com/ZV

Butte Meadows Campground is a great spot to escape into nature without straying too far from creature comforts. Located along rushing Butte Creek and under a canopy of trees, this campground offers a mix of wilderness and convenience. Despite its tranquil, wooded setting, it's close to local amenities - a short stroll will take you to Butte Meadows Mercantile for supplies or to the Bambi Inn for a tasty burger.

The campground has 13 sites, each with a picnic table and fire ring. The campsites and restrooms are well-maintained and clean. While there's some road noise, it's generally not bothersome. The campground is quiet and lightly used mid-week but can get busy on the weekends.

Photos: https://t2bk.com/ZW

*** REDWOOD COAST ***

23. MATTOLE BEACH CAMPGROUND - $15/$7.50

- BLM
- 3750 Lighthouse Road
- Petrolia, CA
- GPS: 40.2892, -124.3559

Map: https://t2bk.com/ZX

Mattole Beach Campground is a must-visit if you're up near California's north coast, even if you don't want to camp there. The beach is long and ideal for walking, exploring, enjoying the dramatic Pacific Ocean surf, or finding that perfect bit of driftwood. 14 tent/trailer campsites with picnic tables, fire rings, vault toilets, and no hookups. Lost Coast Trailhead and parking area. Wheelchair accessible. Sites are closely spaced, but you are right on the beach facing the Pacific Ocean.

This campground is at the north end of the Lost Coast, with a vast roadless area to the south. The road to the campground is long and rough in some places, but there are no problems. It is paved, but I wouldn't advise taking a big rig out there. It's best for tent camping and small campers.

Photos: https://t2bk.com/ZY

24. TRINIDAD SOUTHBOUND REST AREA - FREE

- Rest Area
- Redwood Hwy South
- Trinidad, CA
- GPS: 41.0919, -124.1505

Map; https://t2bk.com/ZZ

Trinidad Southbound Rest Area is located just off I-25 south of Trinidad, Colorado, and provides basic facilities for travelers heading south. The area is set among rolling grasslands with scattered trees, offering some shade and open views of the surrounding hills. It's a quiet stop compared to busier highway rest areas, and a good spot for stretching your legs or taking a short break during long drives. Wildlife such as pronghorn and hawks are occasionally seen in the nearby fields.

Facilities include restrooms, picnic tables, trash bins, and potable water. There are separate parking areas for cars and larger vehicles like RVs and trucks, with enough space for maneuvering. Pets are allowed on leash. This rest area does not allow overnight camping but is open for day use and short stops. Maximum 8 hour stay.

Photos: https://t2bk.com/AAA

25. PANTHER FLAT CAMPGROUND - $15/$7.50

- Six Rivers National Forest
- Redwood Highway
- Gasquet, CA 95543
- GPS: 41.843, -123.929

Map: https://t2bk.com/AAB

Panther Flat is the largest and most popular campground in the Smith River area. It is about 50 feet above the Middle Fork of the Smith River. The campground is along Highway 199 and experiences some road noise during the day, but it's quiet at night. The area is shaded by trees and interspersed with huckleberry bushes, providing privacy between sites.

Photos: https://t2bk.com/AAC

Paved pads and roads, easy river access, trash disposal, potable water, showers, and flush toilets all in a fantastic location. There's a no-fee, day-use area available. The campsites are generously sized with just a short walk to the Smith River. Plus, Redwood National Park is only a short drive away. Given its location and popularity, the campground has many visitors and can get busy in the summer.

26. GRASSY FLAT CAMPGROUND - $10/$5

- Six Rivers National Forest
- Redwood Highway
- Gasquet, CA
- GPS: 41.857, -123.887

Map: https://t2bk.com/AAD

Grassy Flat Campground lies next to the Middle Fork of the Smith River and is bordered by Highway 199. Despite its name, the campground isn't grassy, but it is flat, with plenty of trees providing shade and shrubs offering privacy between sites. The river flows about 50 feet below the campground, and a short walk along a trail leads to a scenic view of the river. The trail also descends to a shallow swimming and fishing spot with a small gravel beach.

The campground has vault toilets, picnic tables, and fire pits, but there's no water available on site. It's an ideal spot for exploring the Smith River area, the magnificent Jedediah Smith Redwoods, and the Oregon Caves National Monument.

Photos: https://t2bk.com/AFY

27. BEAR RIVER CASINO – 72 HOURS FREE.

- Parking Lot
- Fortuna, CA
- GPS: 40.6282, -124.206

Maps: https://t2bk.com/AAF

Parking in their large lot is free for 72 hours with a complimentary player's pass that includes a $10 credit for games. Security patrols and cameras add to the overall sense of safety. The staff is friendly, and the facilities and the parking lot are well-maintained. The on-site restaurant offers good food. This spot is an excellent choice for an overnight stay because of its easy access and cleanliness.

28. JEDEDIAH SMITH CAMPGROUND - $35/$17.50

- Jedediah Smith Redwoods State Park
- U.S. 199
- Crescent City, CA
- GPS: 41.798, -124.0845

Map: https://t2bk.com/AAG

Camp among the towering old-growth redwoods along the wild and scenic Smith River. This spot offers hiking trails, swimming, fishing, and seasonal campfire programs. Cabins are also available for those who prefer a bit more comfort. Jedediah Smith Redwoods State Park has 89 sites, each with a table, fire ring, cupboard, and restrooms nearby. There are no hookups.

Map: https://t2bk.com/AAH

The beauty of this park is truly something to behold. A short walk from your campsite, you will find majestic redwoods and a beautiful rock beach along the gorgeous blue-green Smith River. The restrooms are kept immaculately clean, and hot showers are available. Numerous trails wind through the redwoods, offering a quiet and awe-inspiring experience.

29. SWIMMER'S DELIGHT CAMPGROUND - $30

- Humboldt County Park
- Highway 36
- Carlotta, CA
- GPS: 40.489, -123.9697

Maps: https://t2bk.com/AAI

Tucked away in a shady redwood grove along the Van Duzen River, this family-friendly campground offers a quiet retreat amidst towering trees. It has stunning views, peaceful surroundings, and easy access to the river. In addition to showers, the campground has some of the best trails meandering through old-growth redwoods—a rare find in campgrounds. This spot feels magical.

Photos: https://t2bk.com/AAJ

The campsites are set among the giant redwoods and have tables and fire pits with grills. You can swim in the Van Duzen River or relax at the beach. The bathrooms are clean, with coin-operated showers available. First-come, first-served. Just a half-mile away is the spectacular Cheatham Grove, and three miles down the road, Grizzly Creek Redwoods offers weekend campfire programs.

2

SIERRA NEVADA

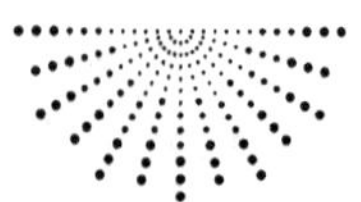

31. LAKES BASIN RECREATION AREA

- Near Graeagle, California
- GPS: 39.7016874,-120.6769558

Map: https://t2bk.com/AAM

Nine miles southwest of Graeagle, California, Lakes Basin is one of Northern California's most beautiful and dramatic areas. Nearby, you will find stunning scenery and over 20 small lakes, most of which you can reach via hiking trails. You'll find a variety of recreational activities, such as camping, fishing, boating, hunting, biking, horseback riding, picnicking, hiking, swimming, windsurfing, and nature study. In the winter, visitors can snowmobile, cross-country ski, and snowshoe.

Lakes Basin Recreation Area includes Gold Lake Campground, Lakes Basin Campground, Packsaddle Campground, Sardine Lake Campground, Goose Lake Campground, Snag Lake Campground, and more.

Photos: https://t2bk.com/AAL

32. GOLD LAKE CAMPGROUND - $22/$11

- Lakes Basin Recreation Area
- Plumas National Forest
- Gold Lake Road
- Graeagle, CA
- GPS: 39.6786, -120.6462

Map: https://t2bk.com/AAN

Gold Lake Campground is located along the shores of Gold Lake at an elevation of 6,400 feet. Eleven of the 37 campsites are available for reservation. The road north of the boat launch facility is narrow and rough, better suited to smaller vehicles and tent campers. The campground is great for boating and fishing.

Photos: https://t2bk.com/AAO

The campsites here are rugged but nice, with many sites near the lake. It's a gorgeous and tranquil area. The lake offers an excellent spot for swimming, and if you're up for a short drive, the Long Lake Trail and Round Lake Trail, both excellent hiking trails, are just 10 minutes away. This spot is part of the Lakes Basin Recreation Area, which includes several other campgrounds, including Packsaddle, Sardine Lake, Goose Lake, and Snag Lake.

33. WATSON LAKE CAMPGROUND - FREE

- Tahoe National Forest
- Watson Lake Rd
- Truckee, CA
- GPS: 39.2239, -120.1377

Map: https://t2bk.com/AAP

Watson Lake Campground is a quiet spot out of the Lake Tahoe hustle. It's a small campground with just 6 spaces along the Tahoe Rim Trail, and there's a small lake with tight camping spots, all on a slope facing the water.

There is only room for very small rigs, but if you have a smaller trailer, you can park your tow vehicle in the day-use area. This area is excellent for kayaking and hiking.

Photos: https://t2bk.com/AAQ

34. ALPINE MEADOW CAMPGROUND - $20/$10

- Army Corps of Engineers
- Martis Dam Rd
- Truckee, CA
- GPS: 39.3206, -120.1224

Map: https://t2bk.com/AAR

Martis Creek Lake has a nice campground off the usual path close to Lake Tahoe, Truckee, and Reno. The area around Martis Creek is perfect for those who love hiking, biking, canoeing, kayaking, and trout fishing. The campground is clean and easy to get to, making it a great middle-ground location that offers quick trips to Truckee or Lake Tahoe.

Photos: https://t2bk.com/AAS

Potable water is available in several spots, along with paved pads and bear-proof dumpsters. This is a good choice if you're looking for a camping spot close to Tahoe but with fewer crowds. A small private plane airport is nearby, so there can sometimes be some noise. The facilities are basic, offering some shade and usually a quiet atmosphere. While weekends tend to be busy, it's rare for the campground to be full.

35. INDIAN VALLEY CAMPGROUND - $24/$12

- Tahoe National Forest
- Indian Valley Road
- Camptonville, CA
- GPS: 39.513, -120.981

Maps: https://t2bk.com/AAT

Indian Valley Campground is about 15 miles north of Camptonville. It is on the north bank of the North Yuba River along Highway 49. The campground is paved and has clean, well-maintained, large sites. The sites are spaced out to ensure privacy, and there are options for sun lovers and shade seekers. It has 19 campsites, vault toilets, and piped water. There are no hookups available.

Maps: https://t2bk.com/AAU

Lying among oak, fir, pine, and madrone trees, the campground has access to the North Yuba Trail and is just 9 miles from Downieville. Facilities include clean pit toilets, fire pits, and picnic tables. Easy river access. It's a popular spot, so it can get quite busy during peak times. A bridge to access the other side of the river is just down the road at Rocky Rest Campground.

36. PACKSADDLE CAMPGROUND - $24/$12

- Tahoe National Forest
- Packer Lake Road
- Sierra City, CA 96125
- GPS: 39.6238, -120.6499

Map: https://t2bk.com/AAV

Packsaddle Campground is located among pine and fir trees, with stunning views of the Sierra Buttes and nearby alpine lakes. With 14 well-developed sites, the campground has piped water and vault toilets. It is surrounded by open meadows dotted with wildflowers, overlooking a ravine set against a backdrop of granite mountains. The area is rich with granitic ridges and glacially shaped rock formations, making for breathtaking scenery.

This campground is suitable for tents, RVs, horses, dogs, and kids. It has a clean outhouse, a hand-operated potable water pump, tables, food lockers, dumpsters, and horse corrals. It's perfect for those who love hiking, biking, horseback riding, boating, and fishing in the surrounding lakes. The elevation is 6,000 feet, so expect cooler temperatures.

Photos: https://t2bk.com/AAW

37. WILD PLUM CAMPGROUND - $24/$12

- Tahoe National Forest
- Wild Plum Road
- Sierra City, CA
- GPS: 39.566, -120.601

Map: https://t2bk.com/AAX

Wild Plum Campground is just a mile east of Sierra City along Haypress Creek off Wild Plum Road. It has 47 campsites, piped water, and vault toilets. The campground is close to the Kentucky Mine and Sierra County Historical Park. It's right by the river and has clean facilities, fantastic hiking trails, and views. Several refreshingly cold swimming holes are within walking distance, and a short hike leads to a beautiful waterfall.

Photos: https://t2bk.com/AAY

Most of the sites at Wild Plum Campground are under a canopy of trees, with dappled sunlight throughout the day. There's a 3-mile loop trail starting right from the campground. This trail winds through the forest, past a waterfall, and along the Pacific Crest Trail (PCT). If you need anything during your stay, Sierra City is nearby, with a small grocery store and a few restaurants.

38. HOPE VALLEY SNOPARK - FREE

- Humboldt-Toiyabe National Forest
- Hope Valley, CA
- GPS: 38.751, -119.94

Map: https://t2bk.com/AAZ

It's peaceful, convenient, and quiet. Hope Valley Sno-Park is located along Blue Lakes Road just off Highway 88 at an elevation of about 7,400 feet. Surrounded by pine, fir, and aspen forest with views of open alpine meadows and nearby peaks, it offers winter access to a range of activities including cross-country skiing, snowshoeing, snowmobiling, and dog sledding. The area is especially popular for its scenic setting and open terrain, making it a favorite spot for winter recreation.

Photos: https://t2bk.com/ABA

Sorenson's is a nice cafe down the road. Gas up before heading to the mountains, as there is no service there. A California Sno-Park permit is required from November 1 through May 30 and must be displayed in each vehicle. Vault toilets are on site, but there is no water Overnight camping in vehicles is allowed, but tent camping is not permitted on paved surfaces.

39. LINDSEY LAKE CAMPGROUND - $15

- PG&E
- FSR 17
- Nevada City, CA
- GPS: 39.413, -120.643

Map: https://t2bk.com/ABB

Lindsey Lake Campground has 12 primitive sites with vault toilets and no trash service, so pack it in/pack it out. The only water available is from the lake, so bring your own. Best for tents, vans, or small cab-over-campers only. No big rigs! It is located bout 12 miles north of Highway 20. Good hiking, fishing, and swimming. There's an informal boat launch, and each campsite has a bench, a fire pit, and a bear box. No reservations. First come, first serve.

The road to get there is a bit rocky, so a high-clearance vehicle is recommended. Once you're there, you can enjoy some excellent day hikes and peaceful fishing. Non-motorized boating only. Lake Lindsey is an ideal trailhead for some truly stunning short backpacking trips in the High Sierra.

Photos: https://t2bk.com/ABC

40. COTTONWOOD CREEK CAMPGROUND - $20/$10

- Tahoe National Forest
- Verdi Grade Road
- Sierraville, CA
- GPS: 39.549, -120.317

Map: https://t2bk.com/ABD

Cottonwood Creek Campground is on Highway 89, alongside the seasonal Cottonwood Creek. It's four miles south of Sierraville and an excellent base for outdoor activities like fishing, hunting, hiking, and biking. The campground is tucked away from the highway, offering a peaceful retreat amidst Jeffrey pine and red and white fir trees. The forest canopy provides shade and privacy between sites.

This campground has clean pit toilets, picnic tables, and spacious sites. The Cottonwood Creek Botanical Trail and Overlook Trail start right within the campground. Sites range from small for tents only to larger for big rigs. If you need supplies or a meal out, Sierraville is close by and has a small gas station/market and restaurants.

Photos: https://t2bk.com/ABE

41. BEARDSLEY DAM CAMPGROUND - $25/$12.50

- Stanislaus National Forest
- Forest Route 5N02
- Tuolumne, CA
- GPS: 38.21, -120.075

Map: https://t2bk.com/ABF

Beardsley Dam Campground is a peaceful and scenic camping area near Beardsley Dam along Forest Road 5N02 at the southern end of Beardsley Reservoir. Each campsite has a picnic table, a metal fire ring, and bear-proof lockers. The campground has potable water, vault toilets, and trash service. The campground is first-come, first-served.

Photos: https://t2bk.com/ABG

With twenty-six individual sites and additional group sites, it's an excellent spot for those seeking a quiet and relaxing escape. Campers will enjoy stunning views of the lake. The campground can accommodate RVs and trailers up to a maximum length of 36 feet, making it suitable for various campers. The beautiful lake offers excellent beach spots and good hiking and fishing.

42. FRASER FLAT CAMPGROUND $25/$12.50

- Stanislaus National Forest
- Forest Route 4N42
- Long Barn, CA 95335
- GPS: 38.17, -120.07

Map: https://t2bk.com/ABH

Frasier Flat Campground is in the Stanislaus National Forest and is super tidy and well-kept. The pit toilets are always clean. The campsites are all flat, and there are a couple of double sites. There are both sunny and shady sites. The south fork of the Stanislaus River runs right alongside the campground, making it perfect for some quality fishing.

Photos: https://t2bk.com/ABI

The campground has a nice hike that follows the river and offers inspiring granite views. The nearby Strawberry Grade trail used to be an old mining railroad, but now it's a nice path for a walk or a bike ride. It's a good place for hanging out, fishing, hiking, or kicking back and enjoying the Sierra's beauty. However, it can get busy on the weekends!

43. HARDIN FLAT ROAD DISPERSED CAMPSITES - FREE

- Stanislaus National Forest
- Hardin Flat Rd
- Groveland, CA
- GPS: 37.8111, -119.9056

Map: https://t2bk.com/ABJ

Dispersed camping. This is not a campground. This campsite is conveniently located just 3 miles from Yosemite's entrance, making it an excellent choice for those wanting to explore the park. Thanks to its clear, open skies, it's excellent if you're using solar. The road to the campsite branches off from the main road and stretches along for a way, so feel free to drive along and pick out your ideal spot. Along Hardin Flat Road, you'll find various camping options, some offering open views while others are in the bush for more privacy.

And here's a quirky detail – if you hear bells during the night, there's no need to worry. It's just the local cows known to wander around the area with cowbells. This site is in Stanislaus National Forest. Free camping very close to the Big Oak Flat Entrance to Yosemite National Park!!

Photos: https://t2bk.com/ABK

44. SWEETWATER CAMPGROUND - $29/$14.50

- Stanislaus National Forest
- CA-120Groveland,
- GPS: 37.8239, -120.0051

Map: https://t2bk.com/ABL

Sweetwater Campground is located in a mixed conifer forest next to Highway 120 and is a stone's throw from Yosemite National Park. It's an ideal spot for exploring Yosemite, and additional day-use options are nearby. The campground offers basic dry campsites, most of which are open and sunny. Each site has a picnic table, a bear-proof storage box, and a fire pit with a grill. Accessible vault toilets and potable water are available from May to September in the summer.

This campground is quiet, and the sites are nicely spaced, offering some privacy. They're not all on level ground, but they're manageable. The bathrooms are kept clean. Not suitable for larger rigs.

Photos: https://t2bk.com/ABM

45. ALABAMA HILLS, MOVIE FLAT DESIGNATED DISPERSED CAMPING - FREE

- Alabama Hills Recreation Area
- BLM
- Lone Pine, CA
- GPS: 36.6054, -118.1189

Map: https://t2bk.com/ABN

Dispersed camping. This is not a campground. The Alabama Hills has spectacular views of Mt. Whitney and this unique desert area. Creeks and waterfalls are nearby. Hundreds of movies have been filmed in this area. Plan to stop at the film museum in Lone Pine.

Recent rule changes make this area more suitable for smaller rigs. Most of the areas that were suitable for bigger rigs are now designated as day use only. The following listing for Tuttle Creek is an excellent option for rigs of all sizes visiting this area. All sites are first-come, first-served. The cover photo for this book was taken here.

Photos; https://t2bk.com/ABO

46. TUTTLE CREEK CAMPGROUND - $10/$5

- BLM
- Horseshoe Meadow Rd.
- Lone Pine, CA
- GPS: 36.5723, -118.1095

Map: https://t2bk.com/ABQ

Tuttle Creek Campground is on the edge of the Alabama Hills and has incredible views of this unique desert area and Mt. Whitney. Tuttle Creek flows through the middle of the campground, and you can find many waterfalls nearby at Whitney Portal and on the way up the mountain. Hundreds of movies have been filmed in this area.

Photos: https://t2bk.com/ABR

Tuttle Creek has 83 RV and tent sites, including ten pull-through spaces. It is suitable for RVs up to 30 feet in length. Each camping spot has a fire pit, picnic table, and lantern holder. No hook-ups are available. Potable water and clean vault toilets are available. There is good cell service. Plan to stop at the Western Film Museum in Lone Pine.

47. GREEN CREEK ROAD DISPERSED CAMPING - FREE

- Toiyabe National Forest
- Green Creek Rd.
- Bridgeport, CA
- GPS: 38.1197, -119.2512

Map: https://t2bk.com/ABS

Green Creek Road dispersed camping is located in the Toiyabe National Forest near Austin, Nevada, offering seclusion within a high desert landscape carved by meadows and intermittent springs. The terrain features open sagebrush flats, scattered pinyon-juniper groves, and gently sloping hills. Spring-fed Green Creek runs nearby, attracting songbirds, deer, and the occasional antelope. While no marked trails begin at camp, forest roads and informal paths lead into adjacent hills and ridgelines, making it appealing for hiking, wildlife viewing, and nature photography.

Camping here is primitive with no designated campsites or amenities. The area accommodates tents and high-clearance trucks or RVs, accessible primarily via forest road. Camping is allowed year-round, with conditions changing by season.

Photos: https://t2bk.com/ABT

48. ASPEN CAMPGROUND - $14/$7

- Inyo National Forest
- Lee Vining, CA
- GPS: 37.939, -119.188

Map: https://t2bk.com/ABU

Aspen Campground is located along Lee Vining Creek in Inyo National Forest at about 7,500 feet elevation. The area is shaded by tall aspen, pine, and fir trees, with many sites close enough to hear the creek. The landscape is a mix of wooded slopes and grassy openings, offering partial views of the surrounding Sierra peaks. Wildlife such as mule deer, marmots, and mountain birds are commonly seen. Fishing for trout is popular along the creek, and several hiking trails in the area lead to alpine lakes and high-country scenery.

Photos: https://t2bk.com/ABV

The campground has 45 drive-in sites, each with a picnic table, fire ring, and bear-proof food locker. Vault toilets are provided, but there is no potable water. All sites are first-come, first-served. The campground can become quite crowded during the summer, but it's a spectacular place to camp. The maximum length allowed for vehicles is 40 ft.

.

49. TIOGA LAKE CAMPGROUND - $28/$14

- Inyo National Forest
- Tioga Road
- Lee Vining,
- GPS: 37.928, -119.255

Map: https://t2bk.com/ABW

Tioga Lake Campground is open seasonally and is located at 9,700 feet. Sites fill quickly. The campground is near Yosemite National Park's Tuolumne Meadows entrance and offers 13 sites by Tioga Lake. You'll enjoy beautiful views of the lake and the surrounding granite mountains.

Remember that you are in bear country. Proper food storage is crucial, and feeding the bears is strictly prohibited. The campground accommodates small RVs or short trailers, but RV hookups are not available.

Photos: https://t2bk.com/ABX

50. GLASS CREEK CAMPGROUND - FREE

- Inyo National Forest
- Glass Creek Rd.
- June Lake, CA
- GPS: 37.7515, -118.9892

Map: https://t2bk.com/ABY

Glass Creek is a very nice free campground. It has a camp host, well-maintained vault toilets, and a good selection of roomy spots. The area has both shady and sunlit sites suitable for solar setups. A rest stop with flushable toilets and potable water is nearby.

The campground is accessible for RVs of all sizes and offers picnic tables, fire rings, and clean toilets. You'll find extensive trails beyond the campsite that are perfect for off-road enthusiasts. It's a 15-minute drive to either Mammoth or June Lake. There's no water or trash disposal at the campsite, but both are available at the nearby rest area.

Photos: https://t2bk.com/ABZ

51. LOWER LEE VINING CAMPGROUND - $14/$7

- Inyo National Forest
- Tioga Road
- Lee Vining, CA
- GPS: 37.9301, -119.1539

Map: https://t2bk.com/ACA

Near Yosemite! Lower Lee Vining Campground is open seasonally at an elevation of 7,300 feet. It offers 51 camping spots. There's no access to potable water in the campground, but about a mile west towards the park, you'll find a water filling station at a large pull-off area. Portable toilets are available. Each site includes a bear-proof locker for safe food storage for basic off-the-grid camping.

Bear Track Creek flows through this campground and is a popular fishing spot. The sites near the creek are notably large. The setting is breathtaking, and the restrooms are well-maintained. The Mobil station at Highways 395 and 120 offers a dump station and a good restaurant.

Photos: https://t2bk.com/ACB

52. MONO CREEK CAMPGROUND $35/$17.50

- Sierra National Forest
- Kaiser Pass Road
- Lakeshore, CA
- GPS: 37.357, -118.994

Map: https://t2bk.com/ACC

Mono Creek Campground is near Kaiser Pass and offers a serene and secluded camping experience. The campsites are located in a tranquil meadow at 7,500 feet near Mono Hot Springs. They offer privacy, shade from Ponderosa pines, picnic tables, grills, bear-proof food storage lockers, and vault toilets. The campground has no water source, but water is available at the High Sierra Ranger Station. Large RVs are not advised.

The campground is near Edison Lake and perfect for exploring Ansel Adams or John Muir Wilderness Areas and Mono Hot Springs' hot mineral baths. The area has hiking, fishing, boating, and horseback riding. Open seasonally from June - September.

Photos: https://t2bk.com/ACD

53. OWENS RIVER RD DISPERSED CAMPING - FREE

- Inyo National Forest
- Owens River Rd.
- Mammoth Lakes, CA
- GPS: 37.737, -118.9677

Map: https://t2bk.com/ACE

This is not a campground. It is an outstanding spot for dispersed camping, and it can accommodate large rigs with various places to set up camp. There is excellent cell reception. You can park wherever you like in this dispersed camping area. Excellent sites are available on both sides of Owens River Road.

No facilities or amenities are available on-site, so being self-contained is essential. A rest stop just half a mile away has clean restrooms, trash dumpsters, and potable water. It's close to Mammoth Lakes and June Lake, and you can choose between shady areas or a sunny spot perfect for solar setups.

Photos: https://t2bk.com/ACF

54. CROWLEY LAKE CAMPGROUND - $10/$5

- BLM
- Crowley Lakes Drive
- Mammoth Lakes,
- GPS: 37.5717, -118.7666

Map: https://t2bk.com/ACG

Crowley Lake Campground has 47 sites suitable for RVs and tents. It's recommended that RVs not exceed 30 feet. Each site has a fire pit, picnic table, and a lantern holder, but there are no hookups. Visitors have access to potable water and well-maintained vault toilets. A dump station is available for a fee of $5.00. For additional amenities, the little town of Crowley is just 2 miles south, and Mammoth Lakes is about 10 miles north.

The campground has views of Crowley Lake and the Glass Mountains to the east, and the Sierra Nevada mountains and McGee Mountain and Canyon are the backdrop to the west. It's popular for fishing, boating, windsurfing, horseback riding, and hiking.

Photos: https://t2bk.com/ACH

55. MAMMOTH LAKES SCENIC LOOP – FREE

- Inyo National Forest
- Mammoth Scenic Loop Rd.
- Mammoth Lakes, CA
- GPS: 37.6839,-118.9946

Map: https://t2bk.com/ACI

Dispersed camping. This is not a campground. While not officially designated as a campground, many obvious camping spots are along both sides of the Scenic Loop. Mammoth Scenic Loop is popular for short-term and long-term stays. Some people stay out there for months while working seasonal jobs in town.

This is true dispersed camping in the national forest. There are no bathrooms, water, electricity, or fire rings. Remember that this area is an active bear area, and you won't find any bear box lockers. Have a method of locking up your food (like a bear-proof cooler) that isn't in your vehicle.

Photos: https://t2bk.com/ACJ

56. TABOOSE CREEK CAMPGROUND - $14

- County Park
- Tinemaha Rd. / Taboose Creek Rd.
- Independence, CA
- GPS: 36.9979, -118.2542

Map: https://t2bk.com/ACK

This is a lovely county park next to a creek. While it can get quite hot during the summer, plenty of smaller trees provide ample shade for setting up chairs or a tent. The park can accommodate any size rig and offers stunning views of the eastern Sierra.

Taboose Creek Campground is quiet and clean. It has vault toilets, picnic tables, grills, fire rings, stream fishing, 35 camp spaces, a water well, and can accommodate larger RVs. No shower facilities are available. Visitors can enjoy hiking on the excellent trails to stretch their legs or enjoy the views. Getting to the park is easy since it's only a mile from Hwy 395.

Photos: https://t2bk.com/ACL

57. SAGEHEN MEADOWS CAMPGROUND - FREE

- Inyo National Forest
- Forest Road 1N02A
- Mammoth Lakes, CA
- GPS: 37.8667, -118.8611

Map: https://t2bk.com/ACM

Dispersed camping. This is not a campground. Sagehen Meadows Campground in the Inyo National Forest is a hidden gem for boondockers. Waking up here means being greeted by the delightful scent of sage and the sweet butterscotch aroma of Jeffrey pines – it's truly an experience for the senses! Watch for the wild horses that sometimes roam around the area. The campground is easily accessible thanks to a usually well-maintained forest service road.

Photos: https://t2bk.com/ACN

Autumn is beautiful, with the aspens painting the landscape in stunning fall colors. Facilities are minimal, with just a pit toilet available, but it's completely free and often peaceful due to its very low usage. This unspoiled camp area offers tranquility, majestic trees, a star-filled sky at night, local wildlife, and the refreshing mountain air. Plus, it's conveniently close to Mono Lake, Lee Vining, and Tioga Pass for those wanting to explore further.

3
CENTRAL CALIFORNIA

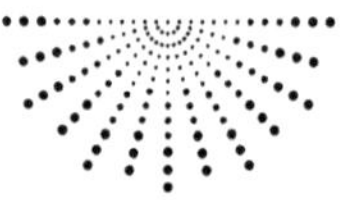

59. CERRO ALTO CAMPGROUND - $35/$17.50

- Los Padres National Forest
- Cerro Alto Rd.
- Atascadero, CA
- GPS: 35.4248, -120.7403

Map: https://t2bk.com/ACO

Tucked in the hills above Morro Bay, this small, basic campground offers 22 sites, 12 of which are accessible to individuals with disabilities. Each site has a picnic table and fire ring, and most have a pedestal grill. Seven sites are available on a first-come, first-served basis. The campground has clean pit toilets in a shady forest not far from the beach.

Photos: https://t2bk.com/ACP

Getting there involves navigating a single-lane road and being cautious of low-hanging branches. The trails starting right from the campground are stunning, winding through trees and shade alongside a creek running through a ravine. It's a short drive to the beach, making it easy for beach visits and exploring Morro Bay. This spot is best suited for tents, truck campers, or very small trailers.

60. BENICIA ENROUTE CAMP - $12

- Benicia State Recreation Area
- Dillon Point Road
- Benicia, CA
- GPS: 38.0787, -122.1943

Maps: https://t2bk.com/ACQ

This spot is ideal for an overnight stay if space is available. Three "Enroute" campsites are available for a night, allocated on a "first-come, first-served" basis. No reservations are available. Each campsite has a bench and a fire pit. The area is perfect for a walk or bike ride to the Bay, and you'll often find people jogging or strolling in the park. This camping site is only for self-contained RVs, and tent camping is prohibited.

The Benicia State Recreation Area features marshlands, grassy hills, and rocky beaches along the narrowest part of the Carquinez Strait. The park is pleasant for picnicking, bird-watching, and fishing and has 2 1/2 miles of road and bike paths. Visitors can bring their dogs to the park but must keep them on a leash.

Photos: https://t2bk.com/ACR

61. MORRO BAY STATE PARK CAMPGROUND - $35

- California State Park
- Morro Bay State Park Rd.
- Morro Bay, CA
- GPS: 35.3465, -120.842

Map: https://t2bk.com/ACS

Morro Bay Campground is perfect for all camping styles, offering over 140 sites for tents, RVs (up to 35 feet with some electrical hookups), and groups. Each spot has a fire ring, picnic table, and nearby water spigots. Facilities include flush toilets, token-operated showers, an RV dump station, and water filling. Activities abound, from hiking and fishing to surfing and wildlife viewing. Plus, it's just a short drive to the beach and downtown. The central coast is an excellent place to cool off in the summer.

Don't miss the Museum of Natural History in Morro Bay State Park, a highlight of California's Central Coast. This educational treasure trove offers nature walks, exhibits, puppet shows, and more. It is suitable for all ages and provides a blend of outdoor adventure and cultural enrichment in one scenic location.

Photos: https://t2bk.com/ACT

62. WILLIAMS HILL RECREATION AREA - FREE

- BLM
- Lockwood San Ardo Rd.
- Bradley, CA
- GPS: 35.9783, -121.0094

Map: https://t2bk.com/ACU

Williams Hill campsites are shaded, with level RV pads, fire rings, shade structures, picnic benches, and vault toilets. There's no electricity, running water, or trash collection services. The campground, maintained by the BLM, stands out for its exceptional views, especially the stunning sunsets and sunrises. Each site has a fire ring, picnic table, and an awning, all in good condition. Pit toilets are available.

The sites are relatively flat, and most are oriented to the west, offering a magnificent view of the sunset over Big Sur. This campground is better suited for smaller rigs.

Photos: https://t2bk.com/ACV

63. SUGARLOAF RIDGE STATE PARK - $35

- California State Park
- Adobe Canyon Rd.
- Kenwood, CA 95452
- GPS: 38.4377, -122.5161

Map: https://t2bk.com/ACW

Sugarloaf Ridge State Park, tucked away in Sonoma County, offers a variety of camping experiences. Suitable for tent camping and RVing, or you can try one of the three glamping sites. They have tent rentals if you need an extra one for the kids. The park has 47 family camping spaces around a large meadow bordered by Sonoma Creek and forested hills. Not far from some great wineries.

Photos: https://t2bk.com/ACX

The campground accommodates RVs up to 31 feet and trailers up to 28 feet. There are water spigots to fill your tanks, but no dump station or hookups. The park offers a peaceful retreat from city life with its dark, quiet nights. Wildlife enthusiasts will enjoy spotting deer, turkeys, and various birds. The drive to the park is a bit of an adventure. It's short but on a narrow, winding road.

64. PRINCESS CAMPGROUND - $34/$17

- Sequoia National Forest
- Highway 180
- Hume, CA
- GPS: 36.8027, -118.9412

Map: https://t2bk.com/ACY

This beautiful campground features three loops: Shining Cloud, Yellow Moon, and Morning Star. There's plenty of shade throughout the site, and privacy varies from fair to good between campsites. Princess Campground is in the heart of Indian Basin Grove, adjacent to Indian Basin Meadow and Creek. It is situated in the Sequoia National Forest and enjoys a cooler climate, even during the warm summer months.

The campground is enveloped by tall trees, with certain areas opening to a vast meadow. At night, the gaps in the treetops create a natural window to the sky above. The forest provides a perfect balance of shade and space so that you can see the starry night sky. Open year-round. First-come, first-served.

Photos: https://t2bk.com/ACZ

65. WESTERN BIG MEADOW ROAD CAMPING AREA - FREE

- Sequoia National Forest
- FR-14S11
- Hume, CA
- GPS: 36.7116, -118.8569

Map: https://t2bk.com/ADA

Dispersed camping. This is not a campground. This excellent free camping area provides easy access to Sequoia and Kings Canyon National Parks. You'll find many camping spots along the road, offering a peaceful and picturesque setting in the woods. This is terrific dispersed camping, with plenty of room to accommodate all sizes of rigs.

Photos: https://t2bk.com/ADB

The road to the area is paved, ensuring easy access to the national parks. Surrounded by forests, there are numerous roads to explore for those seeking adventure. There are pit toilets near the picnic area at the road's entrance. The area has many large, level sites perfect for dispersed camping, including several spots with stunning granite slabs for basking in the sunshine. Note that more free and paid camping areas are to the east on Big Meadow Road.

66. REDWOOD MEADOW CAMPGROUND - $34/$17

- Sequoia National Forest
- Great Western Divide Highway
- Porterville, CA 93257
- GPS: 35.977, -118.592

Map: https://t2bk.com/ADC

This beautiful campground, about 50 miles east of Springville, CA, offers a serene experience. There are vault toilets, but no water, so bring what you'll need. A highlight is the 100 Giants Trail across the road, which features excellent walking trails. For a unique stay, yurts are available for rent at $100 a night.

The campground is known for its quiet and idyllic setting, complete with friendly little critters around. It has excellent views, and campsites have fire pits with grills. Nearby, you'll find great hiking. Most campsites are small, so it's more suitable for small RVs and tent campers. Popular campground.

Photos: https://t2bk.com/ADD

67. UPPER STONY CREEK CAMPGROUND - $34/$17

- Sequoia National Forest
- FR-14S21
- Sequoia National Park, CA
- GPS: 36.668, -118.829

Map: https://t2bk.com/ADE

Upper Stony Creek campground, located 14 miles southeast of Grant Grove on Generals Highway, has sites for RVs and tents. It also has vault toilets, a picnic area, and drinking water. The campground is a good base for hiking into the Jennie Lakes Wilderness or mountain biking in the surrounding areas.

Photos: https://t2bk.com/ADF

Just half a mile away, Stony Creek Resort offers a range of amenities, including a public phone, showers, groceries, Wi-Fi, a restaurant, and gasoline. The drive to the campground can be a bit bumpy. With only 11 sites, the campground feels spacious and quiet. A small river runs near the site, and you can hear the sound of the water at night. It's just 20 minutes from Sequoia National Park.

68. KIRCH FLAT CAMPGROUND - FREE

- Sierra National Forest
- Trimmer Springs Rd.
- Tollhouse, CA 93667
- GPS: 36.879, -119.149

Map: https://t2bk.com/ADG

Kirch Flat Campground is on a large sandy area along the picturesque Kings River. It is surrounded by the gentle hills and oak woodlands of the Sierra Nevada foothills river canyons. Although the summer can be pretty warm, it's a great destination for camping in the spring and fall.

Photos: https://t2bk.com/ADH

It's a favorite among trout fishing enthusiasts, day-trippers, and white-water rafters enjoying the Kings River's challenging rapids and stunning canyon vistas. The campground is remote and quiet. The oak and pine trees scattered across the area offer plenty of shade. There are no water or trash services, so "Pack it In, Pack it Out." Clean pit toilets. Seventeen campsites, a group site, and a raft launch ramp. Due to its remote location, it's important to bring all of the water and food you will need.

69. ACORN CAMPGROUND - $20/$10

- Army Corps Of Engineers
- S Petersburg Rd.
- Valley Springs, CA
- GPS: 38.1764, -120.7995

Map: https://t2bk.com/ADI

Acorn Campground, set in the Sierra Nevada Mountains' brushy hills, is a sunny spot with a warm and dry climate, with summer days often heating up into the 90s. There are 128 campsites. Showers, flush toilets, and drinking water. Year-round fishing for stripers, bass, crappie, bluegill, and catfish. Trails for hiking and biking, plus it's a natural habitat for wildlife like grey foxes, mule deer, coyotes, bald eagles, and mountain lions.

Photos: https://t2bk.com/ADJ

The campground is suitable for tent camping, and several sites are RV-friendly. However, it is not suitable for big rigs. There are no hookups, but there are water spigots, trash cans, toilets and showers, and a dump station. There are also two boat ramps for launching. It is a good place for waterskiing and other water sports.

70. CONDON PEAK CAMPGROUND - $5 PERMIT

- BLM
- Coalinga Rd.
- Coalinga, CA
- GPS: 36.2934, -120.6823

Map: https://t2bk.com/ADK

Condon Peak is a picturesque spot with grassy slopes dotted with tall pines, shrubs, and steeper, rocky areas covered in pine and brush. Newly constructed campsites, RV pads, fire rings, shade structures, picnic benches, and vault toilets. Bring any water you'll need. The campground is accessible via a well-maintained gravel road and offers six beautifully kept sites.

Photos: https://t2bk.com/ADL

The views from Condon Peak are breathtaking. The campsites are private and spacious. Each one includes a sheltered area with a picnic table. Pack-it-in, pack-it-out, and first-come, first-served. The area is excellent for those who love riding, hiking, or just basking in the beauty of nature, with its spectacular views adding to the charm.

71. MCCABE FLAT CAMPGROUND - $10/$5

- BLM Merced River Recreation Management Area
- Briceburg Rd.
- Briceburg, CA
- GPS: 37.5959, -120.0031

Map: https://t2bk.com/ADM

McCabe Flat Campground is located in the Merced River Recreation Management Area. It's 2.3 miles downstream from the Briceburg suspension bridge, on the Wild & Scenic Merced River, and has one of the area's largest sandy beaches. There are vault toilets, dumpsters, and recycling bins.

Photos: https://t2bk.com/ADN

The campground is accessible via the Briceburg River Road, which follows the historical route of the Yosemite Valley Railroad. The dirt and gravel road is manageable for regular passenger vehicles. There are turn-outs along the road. It's an excellent spot for exploring, hiking, fishing, gold panning, and swimming. There are bear-proof lockers, barbecue pits, and convenient access to the river. First-come, first-serve.

72. BUCKHORN RECREATION AREA - $20/$10

- Army Corps Of Engineers
- Buckhorn Road
- Corning, CA
- GPS: 39.8151, -122.371

Map: https://t2bk.com/ADO

This quiet campground in Northern California has beautiful oak-studded grasslands and spring wildflowers. It is located just 10 miles from I-5, with paved county roads for easy access. It's perfect for a peaceful overnight stay with a lake view. Water spigots throughout. Clean restrooms, large showers, and a dump station are available.

Reservations via recreation.gov and cash payments are not accepted on-site. Note that water levels drop in the summer, and this area can be hot. Activities include kayaking, fishing, hiking, biking, and nighttime stargazing.

Photos: https://t2bk.com/ADP

•

73. CARNEGIE SVRA - $10

- California State Park
- Corral Hollow Rd.
- Livermore, CA
- GPS: 37.6312, -121.537

Map: https://t2bk.com/ADQ

Carnegie State Vehicular Recreation Area, located in the hills between eastern Alameda and western San Joaquin counties, is one of California's nine SVRAs managed by the Department of Parks and Recreation. Its location makes it a fantastic base for exploring, especially for those looking to visit the coast, where camping options are limited and pricey.

Photos: https://t2bk.com/ADR

There are showers, and you'll likely get a good cell signal. It's conveniently close to Livermore. Being an off-road recreational area, expect it to be noisy and dusty over the weekends – all part of the fun! Some campsites offer shade, complete with a pergola, picnic table, fire pit, and grill. You'll also find multiple bathrooms on-site, all equipped with running water and electricity.

74. HOLLISTER HILLS SVRA - $10

- California State Park
- Cienega Road
- Hollister, CA
- GPS: 36.7695, -121.4144

Map: https://t2bk.com/ADS

Hollister Hills State Vehicle Recreation Area, California State Parks' first SVRA, is located about an hour south of San Jose. With elevations ranging from 660 to 2,425 feet, it attracts visitors for its natural beauty. The area offers off-highway vehicle (OHV) adventures and designated hiking, biking, and equestrian trails.

Photos: https://t2bk.com/ADT

Camping is first-come, first-served, and there are no designated spots. Facilities include covered picnic tables and fire pits. The first two campgrounds, Radio Ridge and Walnut, are suitable for big rigs. Walnut provides showers, shade, and toilets, while Radio Ridge is perfect for solar power users, with toilet facilities available. The area is especially popular with the dirt bike community, offering an excellent individual and large group camping setup.

75. SELBY CAMPGROUND - FREE

- BLM Carrizo Plain National Monument
- Selby Rd.
- New Cuyama, CA
- GPS: 35.1282, -119.8409

Map: https://t2bk.com/ADU

Located in the Carrizo Plain National Monument, Selby Campground is a free camping spot known for its stunning day and night views. The campground has clean pit toilets and water spigots, although the water supply isn't guaranteed, so it's wise to bring your own. There's no garbage service available, so you'll need to pack out what you bring in. For those with horses, the campground offers three well-maintained pipe corrals.

Photos: https://t2bk.com/ADV

Suitable for tents to RVs of all sizes. In spring, the campground is particularly beautiful, lush, and green, with views of the plains below. Camping is on a first-come, first-served basis. There are 13 basic campsites, each with a picnic table and fire pit. One of the vault toilets is wheelchair accessible. There's unlimited hiking available in the Wilderness Study Area just outside the campground.

76. KCL CAMPGROUND - FREE

- BLM Carrizo Plain National Monument
- Soda Lake Rd.
- Santa Margarita, CA
- GPS: 35.0905, -119.7351

Photos: https://t2bk.com/ADW

Located in the Carrizo Plains, KCL Campground is first-come, first-served, with no reservations. It has twelve campsites, two of which are ADA-compliant, each featuring picnic tables and fire pits. There are horse corrals and an ADA-compliant vault toilet. There's no electricity or drinking water and no garbage service, so be prepared to pack out what you bring in.

You'll travel several miles on a wash-board road, but the destination is well worth it. The area provides good views and nice walking areas. A hiking trail leads up to Caliente Mountain, continues to Selby Campground, and has a great view of the campground area and surrounding plains.

Photos: https://t2bk.com/ADX

77. UPPER SWEETWATER CAMPGROUND - FREE

- BLM Laguna Mountain Recreation Area
- Coalinga Rd.
- Paicines, CA
- GPS: 36.3607, -120.8509

Map: https://t2bk.com/ADY

Located just 25 miles from Pinnacles National Park, this campground offers six well-spaced spots and a clean outhouse. Each campsite is suitable for all sizes of rigs and has shaded picnic tables and fire rings. Please note that there are no garbage facilities, so campers are expected to pack out all their trash. No showers, running water, or electricity are available.

Photos: https://t2bk.com/ADZ

Dispersed camping is not allowed within 200 yards of any wildlife watering area. Campers must park within 15 feet of any roadway when camping or leaving a vehicle. Laguna Creek flows through the area for most of the year, and a series of waterfalls can be found in the Gorge. Although the drive to reach the campground is lengthy and winding, the road is paved, but it's a bit rough.

4
SOUTHERN CALIFORNIA

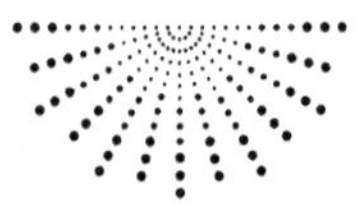

79. GUAJOME REGIONAL PARK - $33

- County Park
- Guajome Lake Rd.
- Oceanside, CA
- GPS: 33.2472, -117.273

Map: https://t2bk.com/AEA

Guajome Regional Park, near Oceanside's coastal community, is a slice of San Diego County's diverse charm. Just 8 miles from the Pacific Ocean, it's an ideal year-round destination near various natural and historic attractions. The park features 4.5 miles of multi-use trails perfect for experiencing its unique habitats like woodlands, chaparral, wetlands, and grasslands. Its two ponds attract migratory birds and offer fishing opportunities for anglers.

Photos: https://t2bk.com/AEB

With thirty-three sites for tents and RVs, Guajome Regional Park is a hub for outdoor activities, including hiking trails that lead to beautiful vantage points. The park has trails and paths that stretch to the ocean. Plus, it's only 15-20 minutes from downtown Oceanside.

80. WILLIAM HEISE COUNTY PARK CAMPGROUND - $29

- County Park
- Heise Park Rd.
- Julian, CA
- GPS: 33.0397, -116.5924

Map: https://t2bk.com/AEC

William Heise Campground in the Laguna Mountain Range is excellent for nature lovers. It is surrounded by oak, pine, and cedar forests near beautiful mountain meadows and a perfect backdrop for nearly 11 miles of scenic hiking and equestrian trails. It's common to spot mule deer, wild turkeys, bobcats, and mountain lions in this area.

Photos: https://t2bk.com/AED

You'll find a variety of camping styles, with cabins, RV sites, tent spots, and a group camp area. Families will appreciate the several playgrounds. There are coin-operated showers and ample picnic spaces, and rangers host weekend activities. The campsites are spacious, shaded, and lovely, with water and electric hookups. At night, the dark sky offers a starry display, enhancing the peaceful and quiet atmosphere of the park.

81. HORSE FLATS CAMPGROUND - $12/$6

- Angeles National Forest
- Silver Moccasin Trail
- Pearblossom, CA
- GPS: 34.3451, -118.0107

Map: https://t2bk.com/AEE

Horse Flats Campground, lies in a shaded area, offers 26 campsites perfect for various outdoor activities. If you're into hiking, the Silver Moccasin National Recreation Trail is easily accessible. The trail also has excellent routes for mountain biking and, true to its name, excellent equestrian facilities, including four corrals and several hitching posts. Each campsite is equipped with picnic tables and campfire rings. There are vault toilets, but no water, so bring what you'll need.

This primitive campground is ideally suited for tent camping. The maximum RV length is 20 feet. During the week, it is very peaceful, making it an ideal getaway. It's a quiet, secluded, off-the-beaten-path destination.

Photos: https://t2bk.com/AEF

82. ALISO PARK CAMPGROUND - FREE

- Los Padres National Forest
- Aliso Park Rd.
- New Cuyama, CA
- GPS: 34.9077, -119.7689

Map: https://t2bk.com/AEG

Aliso Park Campground is peaceful and secluded, surrounded by a creek and ample shade. To reach the area, you'll travel on a paved road through some ranch land, which adds to the peacefulness of the location. There is enough space to accommodate several large rigs, and the campsites are widely spread out.

Photos: https://t2bk.com/AEH

The only restroom available on the site is a porta-potty toilet. Fire permits are mandatory for camping. Campsites are available on a first-come, first-served basis, so you'll want to arrive early to secure a spot.

.

83. OGILBY ROAD DISPERSED CAMPING - FREE

- BLM
- Ogilby Rd.
- Winterhaven, CA
- GPS: 32.9154,-114.8409

Map: https://t2bk.com/AEI

Dispersed camping. This is not a campground. This expansive area includes American Girl Mine Rd, Indian Pass Rd, Tumco Historic Townsite, and more, offering miles of open space perfect for free winter boondocking. Located near the 6-mile marker on Ogilby Road, you'll find an area that's not only wide open but also mostly level, with relatively few RVs around.

Photos: https://t2bk.com/AEJ

There are 3 or 4 roads that branch off Ogilby Road, leading into different camping areas. You can enter through any of these roads to find a suitable spot. The location is perfect for winter boondocking, and whether you have a small or a large rig, finding a place won't be an issue for any size vehicle.

84. OLD ISABELLA ROAD RECREATION SITE - $12/$6

- Sequoia National Forest
- CA-178
- Lake Isabella, CA
- GPS: 35.652, -118.4582

Map: https://t2bk.com/AEK

Situated on Lake Isabella's south side, this camping area provides various amenities, including a vault toilet, trash service, and an information station. The campsites are above the high water mark, offering a good view of the surroundings. Those who prefer to be closer to the water can drive their vehicle to the shoreline and camp at the water's edge.

Photos: https://t2bk.com/AEL

There's a public boat launch, a courtesy dock, and a large, paved parking area suitable for vehicles and boat trailers. There are flush toilets and drinking water. The expansive area provides more space between RVs and more privacy. It's an ideal spot for boating, windsurfing, and kitesurfing. The lake is beautiful, with nice views and sunsets.

85. MT. PINOS CAMPGROUND - $30/$15

- Los Padres National Forest
- Cuddy Valley Rd.
- Frazier Park, CA
- GPS: 34.8106, -119.1091

Map: https://t2bk.com/AEM

Mount Pinos Campground, shaded by Jeffrey Pines, is a cozy spot for campers and RVs (up to 26 feet). It has 19 campsites, picnic tables, fire rings, and vault toilets, but bring your own water. Fifteen sites are available for reservation, while four are on a first-come, first-served basis. The campsites are clean and well-spaced, with dumpsters and pit toilets for convenience. Sites are small, fitting only the smallest trailers.

Photos: https://t2bk.com/AEN

The campground, set among towering pines and refreshing clean air, offers stunning views of Lockwood Valley and Frazier Mountain. It's an excellent spot for enjoying beautiful vistas, hiking, or biking on nearby trails. At night, the sky is a stargazer's dream. It's nice for summer camping or winter snow play. Don't miss the 6.5-mile round-trip hike to Mt. Pinos observatory – it's a highlight.

86. CRYSTAL LAKE CAMPGROUND - $12/$6

- Angeles National Forest
- North Crystal Lake Rd.
- Azusa, CA
- GPS: 34.3242, -117.8353

Map: https://t2bk.com/AEO

Crystal Lake Campground is a gem, and it's just a stone's throw from LA. It's surprisingly affordable, given its location, and offers a gorgeous setting filled with trees. The sites are well-maintained, and you'll have access to running water. It's ok for RVs up to 22 feet, though there aren't any hook-ups.

Maps: https://t2bk.com/AEP

Just across the road is the Crystal Lake Cafe, where you can grab hot meals, sandwiches, and any camping essentials, like firewood. If you're up for outdoor fun, you're right by some fantastic hikes to Mt. Islip and Windy Gap, or you can go fishing in Crystal Lake. The campground is quiet during the week and dog-friendly too. You'll find plenty of shaded spots with water spigots and fire pits, and the trash cans and restrooms are close to all the sites.

87. MOUNTAIN OAK CAMPGROUND - $30/$15

- Angeles National Forest
- Big Pines Hwy.
- Valyermo, CA 93563
- GPS: 34.3945, -117.7293

Map: https://t2bk.com/AEQ

Mountain Oak Campground is northwest of the Los Angeles metro area. It's a scenic and relaxing destination for camping, hiking, picnicking, and wildlife viewing. The campground is suitable for cars, vans, and possibly very small RVs. The campground in the Angeles National Forest is shaded by oak, ponderosa, and sugar pines. This forest, spanning most of the San Gabriel Mountains, provides a striking backdrop for the Los Angeles area.

Photos: https://t2bk.com/AER

You can swim or canoe in Jackson Lake, the only lake near Wrightwood. The lake is stocked with trout and bluegills. Powerboating is not permitted in the lake, so it's peaceful and quiet. You can also hike on the Blue Ridge Trail or the Pacific Crest Trail. Everything you want in a campground: spacious, flat, quiet, beautiful, peaceful, with clean flush toilets. Most of the sites are first-come, first-serve.

88. REYES CREEK CAMPGROUND - $30/$15

- Los Padres National Forest
- Camp Scheideck Rd.
- Maricopa, CA
- GPS: 34.6794, -119.3083

Map: https://t2bk.com/B

Reyes Creek Campground, shaded by oaks and cottonwoods, is a creekside camping spot perfect for escaping it all. It's suitable for RVs up to 22 feet and has 26 campsites, 20 of which are reservable and 6 on a first-come, first-served basis. There are vault toilets. There is no power or water on site. This campground is quite secluded and is about a 40-minute drive from the nearest town, so be sure to plan ahead for gas and supplies.

Photos: https://t2bk.com/atx

Despite being so remote, just outside the campground's entrance is the Camp Scheideck Lodge, a cozy bar and grill serving great food and drinks. Several hiking trails start right in the campground. It's peaceful, with a creek where you can relax by the water. The campground is well-maintained, making it an ideal spot for tent or small-rig camping. It's a natural playground for kids to enjoy splashing in the creek.

89. CAMPO ALTO CAMPGROUND - $30/$15

- Los Padres National Forest
- Hudson Ranch Rd.
- Maricopa, CA
- GPS: 34.8314, -119.2095

Map: https://t2bk.com/AET

Tucked under Jeffrey Pines, Campo Alto Campground is a great spot, and it's suitable for RVs up to 30 feet. There's easy access to the Vincent Tumameit Trailhead. The campground has stunning scenic views, and sites have picnic tables and fire rings. Bring what you need and pack everything out, as no running water or trash cans are available. It's a tranquil mountaintop spot with clean vault toilets, beautiful trees, and fantastic views.

Photos: https://t2bk.com/AEU

It's just a few hours from Los Angeles, but Campo Alto feels secluded and is known for its peace and quiet. It offers dry camping with shaded sites. At an elevation of 8,200 feet, it has breathtaking 360° views of valleys, mountains, and the surrounding landscape. It's a serene and beautiful mountaintop escape.

90. COON CREEK YELLOW POST CAMPSITES - FREE

- San Bernardino National Forest
- FR-1N02
- Angelus Oaks, CA
- GPS: 34.1511, -116.7699

Map: https://t2bk.com/AEV

Coon Creek Yellow Post Campsites offer excellent boondocking, with free camping in a Jeffrey pine forest. No reservations. Quiet and peaceful, with large campsites and beautiful scenery. Each site has a picnic table and a fire ring. Campsites are set far apart for privacy, and hiking trails are nearby.

Access to the first 14 sites is relatively easy for most vehicles. However, sites 15 through 19, further up the road, require a four-wheel drive or a high-clearance vehicle to access. There are no restrooms or water facilities on-site. There's only the nearby creek or Jenks Lake for water, so bring what you need.

Photos: https://t2bk.com/AEW

91. SILURIAN DRY LAKE BED - FREE

- BLM
- Death Valley Rd,
- Baker, CA
- GPS: 35.5266, -116.1785

Map: https://t2bk.com/AEX

Dispersed camping. This is not a campground. Camping at Silurian Dry Lake Bed is like stepping into a world of stunning desolation. It's the perfect spot for boondocking, offering a peaceful retreat in the desert. You're surrounded by breathtaking views that make this a unique experience. Be aware, though, that the desert wind can sometimes be a challenge.

Photos: https://t2bk.com/AEY

Every sunrise and sunset here can be a spectacular show, and the sky is a blanket of stars at night. The silence is profound. If you're lucky, you might see some wild burros. This place is a dream for those who cherish solitude and want to escape it all. There's also plenty to explore nearby, including old turquoise mines, if you do some research to see where they are.

92. TRONA PINNACLES - FREE

- BLM
- Trona, CA
- GPS: 35.619, -117.37

Map: https://t2bk.com/AEZ

Dispersed camping. This is not a campground. The Trona Pinnacles are a marvel of surreal natural beauty in an almost alien landscape. This extraordinary area features over 500 tufa spires, some towering as high as 140 feet, emerging from the Searles Dry Lake floor. Recognizing its unique geological value, the Trona Pinnacles were designated a National Natural Landmark in 1968 by the U.S. Department of the Interior, celebrated as one of North America's most remarkable examples of tufa tower formations.

This unearthly landscape offers an incredible camping, hiking, or off-roading setting. The area is laced with hiking and off-roading trails, which are great for exploration. The Pinnacles can get quite busy on weekends. As of this writing, the smoother access road is from the north via Highway 178 from Searles Valley.

Photos: https://t2bk.com/AFA

93. OWL CANYON CAMPGROUND - $6/$3

- BLM Rainbow Basin Natural Area
- Rainbow-Basin
- Barstow, CA
- GPS: 35.0213, -117.0217

Map: https://t2bk.com/AFB

Own Canyon Campground in Rainbow Basin has a mix of hills, canyons, and washes, making it a hub for various activities like hiking, camping, photography, sightseeing, and horseback riding. The area is known for its multicolored rock walls and mesas, providing plenty of opportunities for photographers. The washes serve as excellent hiking trails. This prime spot for desert boondocking offers large sites and is conveniently located near pit toilets, making it an ideal destination for an overnight stay.

While the 5-mile journey on a washboard dirt road might be challenging, the beautiful desert landscapes waiting at the end make it worthwhile. Each campsite has a fire pit, grill, and covered picnic table. The vault toilets are kept clean, and the sites are generously sized, accommodating everything from tents to larger rigs.

Photos: https://t2bk.com/AFC

94. KELSO DUNES MINE - FREE

- Mojave National Preserve
- Kelso-Dunes Road
- Amboy, CA
- GPS: 34.8881, -115.7166

Map: https://t2bk.com/AFD

Dispersed camping. This is not a campground. This location near the Kelso Dunes is a fantastic boondocking find. It's the perfect place to see the sunrise and sunset over the dunes. While there's no shade, the area's beauty is magical. The ample space has enough room to accommodate multiple vehicles and offers incredible views of the dunes. Pit toilets are available.

The dunes themselves, along with the views and night sky, are breathtaking. Getting there might test your patience due to the road conditions, but the destination is worth the effort. You'll love this spot if you enjoy wide-open spaces and stunning sunrises. It's suitable for rigs of all sizes.

Photos: https://t2bk.com/AFE

95. MID HILLS CAMPGROUND - $20/$10

- Mojave National Preserve
- Wild Horse Canyon Rd.
- Cima, CA
- GPS: 35.1299, -115.4354

Map: https://t2bk.com/AFF

Mid Hills Campground, located at 5,600 feet among pinyon pines and juniper trees, offers an escape from the desert heat below. The unpaved access road is rough, making it unsuitable for larger motorhomes or trailers. It is best for higher-clearance vehicles. The campground has pit toilets, trash receptacles, fire rings, and picnic tables.

Photos: https://t2bk.com/AFG

It is very secluded and has fantastic views. It has a quiet and peaceful atmosphere. Beautiful sunrises and sunsets, as well as the moon and starry night sky, are breathtaking. The restrooms are well-maintained, and the juniper trees and desert flora provide privacy between the large sites. Cima Dome and the Kelso Dunes recreation areas are nearby.

96. FOSSIL FALLS DRY LAKE BED - FREE

- BLM
- Cinder Road
- Little Lake, CA
- GPS: 35.9828, -117.9004

Map: https://t2bk.com/AFH

Dispersed camping. This is not a campground. Fossil Falls Dry Lake Bed is next to the BLM Fossil Falls Recreation Area, which offers stunning scenic views. After exiting the paved road, you will travel a few hundred yards on a bumpy but hard-packed road. You can choose where to set up camp when you reach the lake bed. Very few people use this area.

Although summer can be hot, the rest of the year has pleasant weather. You can also take a leisurely walk to see the Fossil Falls. The cell service at this location is excellent.

Photos: https://t2bk.com/AFI

97. AMBOY CRATER - FREE

- BLM Mojave Trails National Monument
- Crater Road
- Amboy, CA
- GPS: 34.5577, -115.7769

Map: https://t2bk.com/AFJ

Amboy Crater, an iconic landscape of ash and cinders, is one of the United States' youngest volcanic fields. It stands 250 feet tall and has a diameter of 1,500 feet. Just off Old Route 66, this site has picnic tables, restroom facilities, and an ADA-compliant ramada overlook for scenic viewing. There's a hiking trail to the rim, complete with rest stations along the way. The area is very quiet except for the occasional passing train in the distance.

Photos: https://t2bk.com/AFK

The road is easy to navigate in vehicles of any size. Waking up to the lunar-like landscape is a unique experience. The location is exceptionally dark and fantastic for quiet stargazing. The large and level parking lot is perfect for a night under the stars. There are covered picnic tables and two bathrooms with pit toilets on-site. It can get quite hot in the summer but is pleasant the rest of the year.

98. LITTLE COWHOLE MOUNTAIN - FREE

- Mojave National Preserve
- Baker, CA
- GPS: 35.2396, -116.0683

Map: https://t2bk.com/AFL

Dispersed camping. This is not a campground. This spot is an ideal overnight destination, offering top-notch boondocking in a super quiet setting, complete with fire pits. It's convenient as an emergency sleeping spot, always ready when needed. Be prepared for soft spots, potholes, and washboard conditions on the way in and around the camping area.

Photos: https://t2bk.com/AFM

The road's condition is something to be mindful of, but it's manageable for rigs of any size. For amenities, dump and water are available at the Shell station in Baker for $5. Located conveniently close to Baker, it has good cell coverage. Don't miss the chance to explore the Mojave Desert Lava Tube, where you can climb inside.

99. WILDROSE CAMPGROUND - FREE

- Death Valley National Park
- 24 Wildrose Canyon Rd.
- Death Valley, CA
- GPS: 36.2657, -117.1905

Map: https://t2bk.com/AFN

Wildrose Campground is a beautiful spot to camp in Death Valley. The campsites are small and high enough in elevation not to be too warm, but no shade is available. Two roads lead up to the campsite. Emigrant Road has a 25-foot maximum tow restriction. The road is easy until right before the campground when it gets twisty and tight. Wildrose Road is shorter but only partially paved.

Photos: https://t2bk.com/AFO

The road is rugged and not suited to bigger rigs. However, you'll enjoy the gorgeous night sky and vast open space. There are clean bathrooms, water, and trash cans, and each site has a picnic table and spectacular views. There are 23 campsites, and they are available on a first-come, first-served basis.

100. STOVEPIPE WELLS CAMPGROUND - $14/$7

- Death Valley National Park
- Cottonwood Canyon Rd.
- Stovepipe Wells, CA
- GPS: 36.6068, -117.1478

Map: https://t2bk.com/AFP

Enjoy basic camping in the heart of a magnificent National Park, available seasonally from October 15th. Stovepipe Wells campground is at sea level and operates on a first-come, first-served basis. It offers scenic views of Death Valley and the Mesquite Flat Sand Dunes. The campground is next to the Stovepipe Wells general store, a ranger station, and a privately run RV park.

Stovepipe Wells Campground offers dry camping in a large parking area and has flush toilets, trash and recycling bins, dump station access, and potable water refilling. For those interested in hiking, the nearby dunes are a fantastic spot for a morning or evening adventure.

Photos: https://t2bk.com/AFQ

101. FURNACE CREEK ROAD DISPERSED CAMPING - FREE

- BLM
- Furnace Creek Washington Rd.
- Shoshone, CA
- GPS: 35.9061, -116.2968

Map: https://t2bk.com/AFR

Dispersed camping. This is not a campground. South of Death Valley, off of Hwy 127, is an excellent area for stargazing and boondocking. It offers privacy and spaciousness, with room between campsites. The landscapes and views here are breathtaking, with beautiful sunrises and sunsets. There's ample parking available on solid, rocky ground in a beautiful, open area. The terrain is pretty level and clean, but there's no shade.

Photos: https://t2bk.com/AFS

The nights are quiet, perfect for enjoying the expansive sky views. There are no amenities. The dirt road leading to the camp area is well-maintained. The area's landscape and geology offer endless hiking opportunities and rockhounding. The Tecopa hot springs are nearby, as is the China Date Ranch and their delicious date smoothies and shakes.

102. JOSHUA TREE SOUTH DISPERSED CAMPING - FREE

- BLM
- Cottonwood Spring Rd.
- Chiriaco Summit, CA
- GPS: 33.6745, -115.8019

Map: https://t2bk.com/AFT

Dispersed camping. This is not a campground. Joshua Tree South is located a mile from the Cottonwood Springs Rd. exit off I-10, and the lack of road noise makes for a quiet stay. It's only a few miles to Joshua Tree National Park's southern entrance, and there's excellent cell service. The area is gorgeous in the spring when wildflowers bloom. The transformation of the desert during that time of year is breathtaking.

Photos: https://t2bk.com/AFU

The area can accommodate rigs of all sizes. Despite the bumpy dirt road, it's easy to navigate to this location with a regular car. There are no facilities here, but there is a dump station at Joshua Tree NP's Cottonwood campground. Great for star gazing.

103. BELLE CAMPGROUND - $25/$12.50

- Joshua Tree National Park
- Belle Campground Rd.
- Twentynine Palms, CA
- GPS: 34.0021, -116.021

Map: https://t2bk.com/AFV

Belle Campground is small, with 18 sites and first-come, first-served. Be sure to bring plenty of your own water, as none is available on-site, though pit toilets are provided. This campground is great for stargazing, thanks to the dark night skies it offers. The campsites are cleverly situated among the rocks, creating a picturesque Joshua Tree setting with large granite boulders and the iconic Joshua trees dotting the landscape.

It's smaller, more secluded, and quieter than other Joshua Tree campgrounds. Its central location offers easy access to many of the park's main attractions. The area is known for its incredible sunsets and sunrises, breathtaking starry skies, beautiful rock formations, and the call of coyotes at night.

Photos: https://t2bk.com/AFW

5
BLM WINTER AND SUMMER LONG-TERM VISITOR AREAS

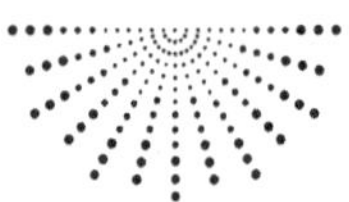

Visitors may or may not consider these 5-star camping areas, but they are worth knowing about. They are very inexpensive and convenient for full-timers, long-timers, and snowbirds.

THERE ARE SEVEN WINTER LTVAS

LTVA Details: https://t2bk.com/AFX

A recreation permit is needed during the LTVA winter season, or any part of the 7 months from September 15th to April 15th. For those staying longer than 14 days, a long-term LTVA permit is priced at $180 for up to 7 months. If you're planning a shorter visit, a 14-day permit is available for $40, valid from the date of purchase. In the off-season, from April 16th to September

14th, you can camp free, but the standard 14-day limit for dispersed camping on BLM land is in effect. Your winter recreation permit is valid at any of the following LTVAs. And yes, you can move from one to another on the same permit.

Hot Spring LTVA Between El Centro, CA and Yuma, AZ

Tamarisk LTVA Between El Centro and Yuma

Pilot Knob LTVA just west of Yuma, AZ

Midland LTVA is about 7 miles north of Blythe, CA

Mule Mountain LTVA is 10 miles south of I-10. There are two campgrounds at Mule Mountain LTVA: **Coon Hollow,** with 28 campsites, and **Wiley's Well,** with 14 campsites

There are two winter LTVAs just over the border in Arizona:

La Posa LTVA is about 2 miles south of Quartzsite

Imperial Dam LTVA is 20 miles north of Yuma, AZ

THERE ARE FOUR SUMMER LTVAS IN CALIFORNIA

The summer LTVAs are located on the eastern side of the Sierras, just off Highway 395. A long-term permit is valid for the entire season or any part of it. The season is from the first Saturday in March through November 1st and is valid for all summer LTVAs in California. The cost is $300. You can also buy a one-month pass for $100. You must purchase these passes at the BLM Field Office in Bishop, CA. As of this writing, passes are only available on Mondays from 8 am to 12 noon.

Crowley Lake LTVA is about 10 miles south of Mammoth Lakes

Goodale Creek LTVA is between Bishop and Lone Pine

Tuttle Creek LTVA is just outside of Lone Pine

Horton Creek LTVA is about 12 north of Bishop.

All of these LTVAs are easily found on Google Maps, or use the QR code on the previous page.

6
RESOURCES

RESOURCES FOR THOUSANDS OF GREAT PLACES TO CAMP

These three are my go-to sites and apps to discover places to camp. I highly recommend further research on any camping area to get the latest info on seasonal closing, road or fire damage, etc.

www.campendium.com

Campendium.com is a comprehensive online resource designed for camping and RV enthusiasts to find, review, and share information about campgrounds and RV parks across the United States and Canada. You'll find detailed campground information, photos, reviews, and a convenient mobile app.

www.freecampsites.net

Freecampsites.net is an online resource that helps campers, and RVers find free and low-cost campsites across the United States and Canada. The platform offers a user-generated database of campgrounds, including reviews, GPS coordinates, and essential information to facilitate budget-friendly camping experiences.

www.ioverlander.com

iOverlander.com is a global online platform and mobile app designed for overlanders, campers, and travelers to find and share information about accommodations, camping spots, points of interest, and essential services, fostering a collaborative community for adventure-seekers worldwide.

GOVERNMENT WEBSITES FOR FURTHER RESEARCH

BLM - Bureau of Land Management www.blm.gov

U.S. Forest Service www.fs.usda.gov

Reserve America www.reserveamerica.com

Recreation.gov www.recreation.gov

Discount Passes https://store.usgs.gov/senior-annual

7
THANK YOU!

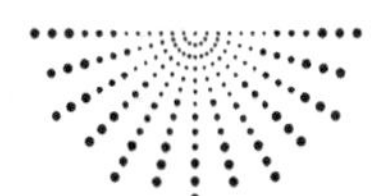

Click or Scan to get notified about my next free and cheap camping book. https://amzn.to/44VJ5EG

I hope you have enjoyed this book, and it has given you a good idea of the vast choices you'll have in finding beautiful, secluded locations to camp on public land in California. Choices that won't break the bank. Choices that mean you can camp longer while spending less money. Thank you for reading. I hope you can get out there soon and have some new adventures!

To get notified when my next "free and cheap camping" book is available on Amazon, click the "Follow" button on the linked page above.

Please leave a review on Amazon!

Enjoying this Book? Please leave a review

Leave a review: https://t2bk.com/aty

The Free and Super Cheap Camping series is your passport to budget-friendly adventures across America's most beautiful public lands in:

COLORADO, UTAH, NEVADA, CALIFORNIA, OREGON, WASHINGTON, ARIZONA, NEW MEXICO

Each book features top-rated campsites, plus the tools and knowledge to help you discover thousands more. Whether you're camping in the mountains, by the sea, or in the desert, you'll find detailed information, GPS coordinates, maps, and tips to help you explore with confidence — all while keeping your travel costs low and your sense of freedom high.

SCAN OR CLICK BELOW TO SEE THE ENTIRE SERIES, AND START PLANNING YOUR NEXT CAMPING ADVENTURE.

Free and Super Cheap Camping Series: https://t2bk.com/ATT

www.ingramcontent.com/pod-product-compliance
Lightning Source LLC
LaVergne TN
LVHW010840120826
845149LV00017B/3332

* 9 7 9 8 9 8 9 7 4 2 0 0 4 *